YORK NOTES

GREAT EXPECTATIONS

CHARLES DICKENS

NOTES BY DAVID LANGSTON
AND MARTIN J. WALKER

 Longman

 York Press

YORK PRESS
322 Old Brompton Road, London SW5 9JH

PEARSON EDUCATION LIMITED
Edinburgh Gate, Harlow,
Essex CM20 2JE, United Kingdom
Associated companies, branches and representatives throughout the world

First published 1997
This new and fully revised edition first published 2002
Second impression 2003

10 9 8 7 6 5 4 3 2

ISBN 0-582-50618-2

Designed by Michelle Cannatella
Illustrated by Chris Brown
Map by Neil Gower
Typeset by Land & Unwin (Data Sciences), Bugbrooke, Northamptonshire
Produced by Pearson Education Asia Limited, Hong Kong

CONTENTS

PREFACE

York Notes are designed to give you a broader perspective on works of literature studied at GCSE and equivalent levels. With examination requirements changing in the twenty-first century, we have made a number of significant changes to this new series. We continue to help students to reach their own interpretations of the text but York Notes now have important extra-value new features.

You will discover that York Notes are genuinely interactive. The new **Checkpoint** features make sure that you can test your knowledge and broaden your understanding. You will also be directed to excellent websites, books and films where you can follow up ideas for yourself.

The **Resources** section has been updated and an entirely new section has been devoted to how to improve your grade. Careful reading and application of the principles laid out in the Resources section guarantee improved performance.

The **Detailed summaries** include an easy-to-follow skeleton structure of the story-line, while the section on **Language and style** has been extended to offer an in-depth discussion of the writer's techniques.

The Contents page shows the structure of this study guide. However, there is no need to read from the beginning to the end as you would with a novel, play or poem. Use the Notes in the way that suits you. Our aim is to help you with your understanding of the work, not to dictate how you should learn.

Our authors are practising English teachers and examiners who have used their experience to offer a whole range of **Examiner's secrets** – useful hints to encourage exam success.

The General Editor of this series is John Polley, Senior GCSE Examiner and former Head of English at Harrow Way Community School, Andover.

The authors of these Notes are David Langston and Martin J. Walker. David Langston (MA) is an English teacher and examiner at GCSE and A level. He has written and contributed to GCSE textbooks. Martin Walker is an English teacher, journalist and AQA examiner at GCSE and A level.

The edition used in these Notes is the Penguin Classics Edition, 1996, edited by Charlotte Mitchell.

PART ONE

INTRODUCTION

HOW TO STUDY A NOVEL

A novelist starts with a story that examines a situation and the actions of particular characters. Remember that authors are not photographers, and that a novel never resembles real life exactly. Ultimately, a novel represents a view of the world that has been created in the author's imagination.

There are six features of a novel:

1 THE STORY: this is the series of events, deliberately organised by the writer to test the characters

2 THE CHARACTERS: the people who have to respond to the events of the story. Since they are human, they can be good or bad, clever or stupid, likeable or detestable, etc. They may change too!

3 THE VIEWPOINT/VOICE: who is telling the story. The viewpoint may come from one of the characters, or from an omniscient (all-seeing) narrator, which allows the novelist to write about the perspectives of all the characters

4 THE THEMES: these are the underlying messages, or meanings, of the novel

5 THE SETTING: this concerns the time and place that the author has chosen for the story

6 THE LANGUAGE AND STYLE: these are the words that the author has used to influence our understanding of the novel

To arrive at the fullest understanding of a novel, you need to read it several times. In this way, you can see how all the choices the author has made add up to a particular view of life, and develop your own ideas about it.

The purpose of these York Notes is to help you understand what the novel is about and to enable you to make your own interpretation. Do not expect the study of a novel to be neat and easy: novels are chosen for examination purposes, not written for them!

EXAMINER'S SECRET
Some knowledge of nineteenth-century England would really help your study of the novel.

AUTHOR – LIFE AND WORKS

1812 Charles John Huffam Dickens is born 7 February at Landport (Portsmouth)

1824 Dickens is put to work at a shoe-blacking warehouse. His father is imprisoned for debt and the rest of the family joins him in Marshalsea Prison

1827–8 Dickens is a solicitor's clerk – he learns shorthand

1829–31 Works as a court reporter. Dickens is a regular reader at British Museum

1831–2 Dickens reports on Parliament. Here he gains a detailed knowledge of London and its inhabitants. His interest in drama develops

1833–6 First story published, 'A dinner at Poplar Walk'. Reporter for *Morning Chronicle*. Dickens becomes engaged to Catherine Hogarth, daughter of George Hogarth, editor of *Evening Chronicle*. *Sketches by Boz* is published. *Pickwick Papers* begins publication in monthly parts. Dickens marries Catherine Hogarth.

1837–40 *Oliver Twist* is published in parts in *Bentley's Miscellany* magazine. *Nicholas Nickleby* begins in monthly parts in April 1838. His new magazine, *Master Humphrey's Clock* (*MHC*), is published. *The Old Curiosity Shop* begins in *MHC*

1841–6 *Barnaby Rudge* begins in *MHC*. Dickens travels with Catherine in United States and Canada. *American Notes* published. *Martin Chuzzlewit* and *A Christmas Carol* are published. The Dickens family travel to

CONTEXT

1812 Napoleon invades Russia

1812–14 War between England and the United States

1815 Napoleon is defeated at the Battle of Waterloo. Corn Laws passed

1820 George III dies. George IV becomes king

1830 George IV dies; his brother William IV becomes king. Manchester–Liverpool Railway opened

1833 Slavery abolished throughout the British Empire

1834 New Poor Law. Houses of Parliament burn down

1837 William IV dies; succeeded by his niece, Victoria

1840 Queen Victoria marries her cousin Albert. Penny post started. Morse invents the telegraph

1842 Chartist Riots

1845–6 Potato crop fails in Europe; famine in Ireland. Corn Laws repealed

AUTHOR – LIFE AND WORKS	**CONTEXT**

Italy. *The Cricket on the Hearth* is published in December. The Dickens family moves to Lausanne in Switzerland and then to Paris. *Dombey and Son* is started

1847–50 The family returns to London. Dickens directs and acts in amateur plays in London, Manchester, Edinburgh and Glasgow. *The Haunted Man* is published as another Christmas book. *David Copperfield* begins in monthly parts

1849 Gold discovered in California and Australia

1850 Telegraph cable laid under English Channel

1851–4 *Bleak House* published. *A Child's History of England* is written. Dickens gives his first public reading from his novels in December in Birmingham. *Hard Times* is published weekly

1851 The Great Exhibition at the Crystal Palace

1853–6 Crimean War

1855–8 *Little Dorrit* is published. Dickens and family move to Gad's Hill. Dickens separates from his wife

1857–8 The Indian Mutiny

1859–62 Dickens continues to give popular public readings. *A Tale of Two Cities* is written. *Great Expectations* is published (1860)

1861 Albert dies; Victoria retires into mourning

1861–5 American Civil War

1863–6 Dickens is in poor health. He continues to give public readings in Paris and London despite warnings from his doctor

1867–9 Dickens tours America, reading from his works. His health worsens. *Mystery of Edwin Drood* is begun

1867 Disraeli's government passes the Second Reform Bill which gives many working men the vote

1870 Dickens gives his final series of readings in London. He suffers a stroke on 8 June at Gad's Hill. Dies 9 June. 14 June Dickens is buried in Westminster Abbey

1869 Suez Canal opened

EXAMINER'S SECRET
You will gain more credit if you show you have some understanding of the novel in its historical context.

SETTING AND BACKGROUND

INDUSTRIAL REVOLUTION

Charles Dickens was born into times that saw great changes in the ways that people lived. The population still lived mainly in the countryside, but the industrial revolution, which had been underway for about sixty years, led to the rapid growth of cities. The growth was so rapid that the housing available to the poor was often appalling. Whilst many people worked long hours in dangerous factories and then went home to squalor, the wealthy few percent of the population lived in luxury.

FEAR OF REVOLUTION

A similar situation had led to revolution in France in 1789. Britain and much of Europe had been at war with the armies of revolutionary France for nineteen years when Charles Dickens was born, and this war was to rage for a further three years until the defeat of Napoleon at Waterloo in 1815. The British government feared revolution at home and so maintained a very harsh regime. The army was called in to deal with any public gatherings which might become unruly. People could be imprisoned without trial. Public executions and transportation to the colonies were used extensively.

TRANSPORTATION

The sentence of banishment from England had been introduced as early as 1597. After the loss of the American colonies in 1788, Australia was used as the main destination for convicts sentenced to transportation. Most of those transported were poor, uneducated people accused of theft. Between 1788 and 1868, 162,000 convicts (137,000 male, 25,000 female) were transported, mainly to New South Wales. Those who suffered this punishment were never meant to return home.

DID YOU KNOW?
Dickens' own experience of poverty clearly shaped his views.

DICKENS' DESIRE FOR CHANGE

The 1800s were years of great prosperity for some in Britain. The new wealth generated by industry and the colonies was shared out amongst a privileged few. The gap between the rich and the poor grew and there were effectively two nations living in Britain.

Dickens was very interested in bringing about change and his novels dealt with such topics as justice and punishment (e.g. *Oliver Twist, Great Expectations*), the harsh treatment of children (e.g. *Nicholas Nickleby*) and the evils of the factory system (e.g. *Hard Times*). He campaigned long and hard against public executions, using his fame to bring the horrors of the situation to light.

Social change did come about during the lifetime of Charles Dickens. New laws were passed to curb the terribly long hours that factory workers had to endure. Young children were prevented from working in factories altogether. The Public Health Act of 1848 began the move towards improved sanitation and public health.

Dickens was an influential voice for thirty-five years and saw some of his ideas about social reform put into practice.

Great Expectations is set in an England of slightly earlier times than the ones in which Dickens actually lived, e.g. in the novel there are no railways.

**CHECK
THE NET**
Find out more about
the life and times of
Dickens at www.
dickensmuseum.
com

CHARLES DICKENS' BACKGROUND

Charles Dickens was born in 1812 in Portsmouth. He was the eldest son and one of eight children, two of whom died in childhood. His father, John Dickens, was a clerk in the Navy Pay Office. He did not manage his money well, got into debt and was sent to Marshalsea Prison. He was soon joined there by his wife and five other children. Charles was taken out of school in London and put to work in a filthy warehouse where he had to stick labels on bottles of boot-black. The family had been forced to sell all of their possessions and Charles felt shamed by this. He returned to school for a short time, but this experience left its mark on Dickens. Even years later, he could not bear to talk about it and many of Dickens' ideas about social conscience probably stem from this episode in his life.

Dickens taught himself shorthand and, by the age of sixteen, was working as a court reporter. This job allowed him to see, first hand, the harsh system of justice which then operated in England. Dickens tired of this dull work and became a newspaper reporter, commenting on Parliament. His newspaper work gave him a detailed knowledge of

London and its inhabitants, both rich and poor, and he was to make use of this in many of his novels and stories.

Dickens became interested in literature and in 1832 he began writing sketches and stories about London life. These began to be published in 1833 and were published together in 1836 as *Sketches by Boz*. This sold so well that Dickens was asked to write some more sketches. This project developed into *The Posthumous Papers of the Pickwick Club*, which appeared as a monthly serial. This form of serial publication was used a great deal by Dickens.

EXAMINER'S SECRET

If you can take your own annotated copy of a text into the exam, be sure that your notes comply with the exam board's regulations.

Charles Dickens never forgot his early brush with English justice and many of his works deal with the problems of growing up in poverty.

He became a very successful author and was famous in both England and America. When the episodes of *Oliver Twist* surrounding the death of Nancy were published there were crowds on the dockside in New York, eagerly wanting to buy the latest instalment. Dickens also gave public readings from his works and these were hugely popular. His wealth allowed him to buy a large house, Gad's Hill, outside London, near countryside like that described in the opening section of *Great Expectations*.

The pressures of touring and the strain of putting great efforts into his public readings began to tell on Dickens and his doctors warned him to stop. He ignored their advice and his health deteriorated. He died in 1870, following a collapse at Gad's Hill.

Now take a break!

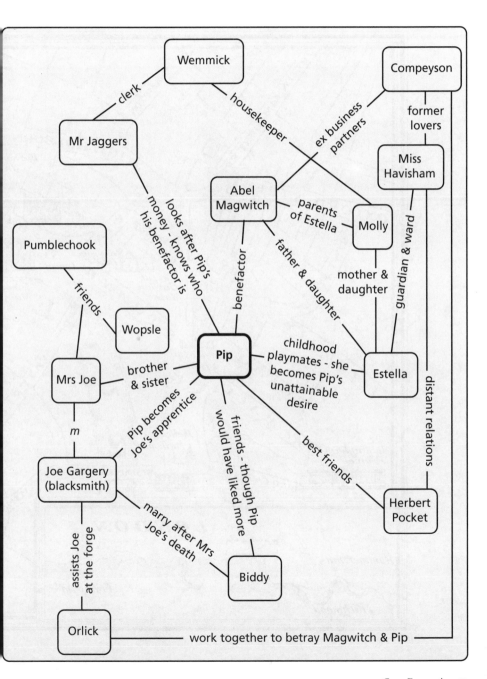

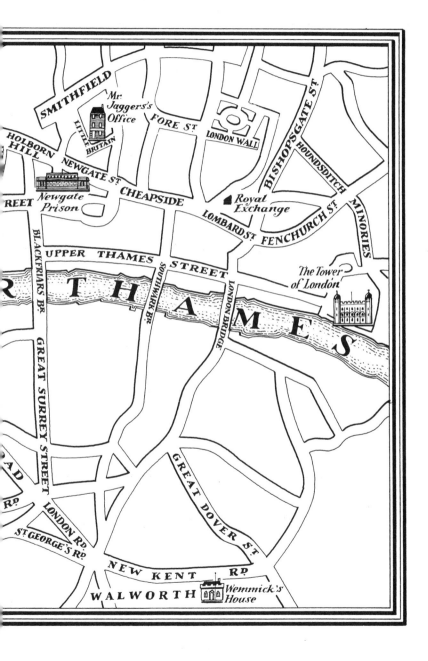

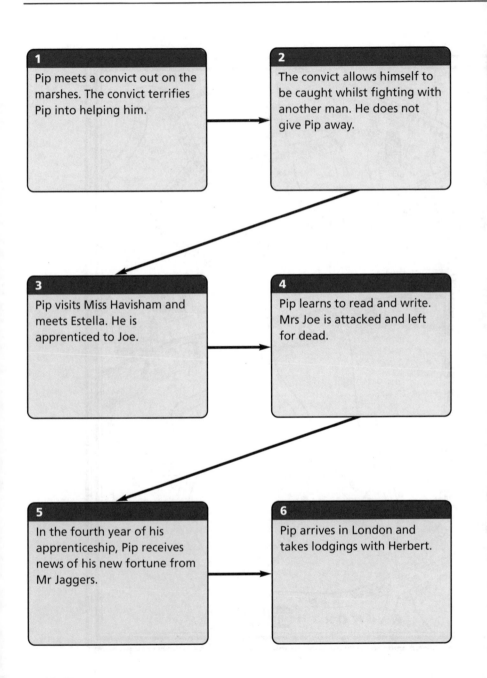

1

Pip meets a convict out on the marshes. The convict terrifies Pip into helping him.

2

The convict allows himself to be caught whilst fighting with another man. He does not give Pip away.

3

Pip visits Miss Havisham and meets Estella. He is apprenticed to Joe.

4

Pip learns to read and write. Mrs Joe is attacked and left for dead.

5

In the fourth year of his apprenticeship, Pip receives news of his new fortune from Mr Jaggers.

6

Pip arrives in London and takes lodgings with Herbert.

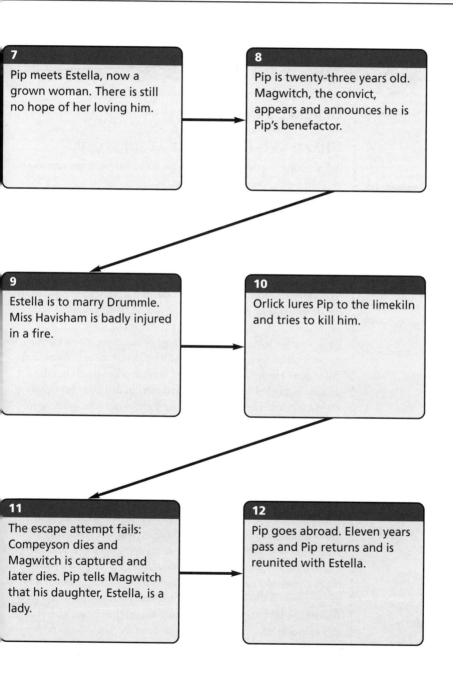

7

Pip meets Estella, now a grown woman. There is still no hope of her loving him.

8

Pip is twenty-three years old. Magwitch, the convict, appears and announces he is Pip's benefactor.

9

Estella is to marry Drummle. Miss Havisham is badly injured in a fire.

10

Orlick lures Pip to the limekiln and tries to kill him.

11

The escape attempt fails: Compeyson dies and Magwitch is captured and later dies. Pip tells Magwitch that his daughter, Estella, is a lady.

12

Pip goes abroad. Eleven years pass and Pip returns and is reunited with Estella.

PART TWO

SUMMARIES

GENERAL SUMMARY

CHAPTERS 1–19: PIP'S LIFE AT THE FORGE

Pip, a young boy of eight or nine, meets a convict in the churchyard near the boy's home on the Thames marshes. Pip says that he lives with his sister and her husband, who is the local blacksmith. The convict is in irons and is hungry and so he makes the boy bring him a file and some food. Pip steals the items and takes them to the convict who then disappears. As the food is missed from the house, soldiers looking for two escaped convicts arrive and seek the help of Joe, the blacksmith. Out on the marshes they track Pip's convict who is found fighting with another escaped prisoner and is so determined not to let the other prisoner go that both men end up being caught.

Pip is sent for to go and play at a large house in the town. He finds the house is called Satis House and that it has a very strange inhabitant called Miss Havisham. She is an old woman who spends her days dressed in a faded wedding dress and surrounded by other decaying wedding items. The rooms she occupies have not seen daylight for many years and neither has she. There is also Estella, a girl of around Pip's age, whom Miss Havisham asks to play cards with Pip. Estella delights in humiliating the boy, but he finds her beautiful anyway.

A strange visitor to town gives Pip two pound notes and the man clearly has some connection with Pip's convict as he stirs his drink with the same file Pip has stolen. Pip meets the Pockets at Miss Havisham's and a strange boy makes Pip fight with him. Miss Havisham pays Joe to take Pip on as his apprentice and so he is sworn to the trade of blacksmith. In the meantime, Pip attends a poorly run night class in the town where he meets Biddy, a bright girl of a similar age to himself. Pip is not satisfied with his position in life and feels that he should be destined for greater things than being a blacksmith. Pip's sister is attacked and injured so severely that she can no longer speak. Pip suspects Orlick, Joe's assistant, who argued with his sister earlier the same day.

A stranger arrives from London and announces himself as Mr Jaggers, a lawyer. Pip has seen him before at Satis House. He tells Pip that the boy is to inherit a large property and that he must go to London immediately to begin his training in life as a gentleman. As a condition, Pip is not to try to find out who his mysterious benefactor is. He assumes that it is Miss Havisham. Pip goes to London, leaving Joe and Biddy behind.

CHAPTERS 20–39: PIP IN LONDON

In London, Pip begins his education with Mr Matthew Pocket, a cousin of Miss Havisham, and strikes up a close and lasting friendship with his son Herbert. He shares rooms with Herbert at Barnard's Inn.

Pip learns that his guardian, Jaggers, inspires fear and respect amongst the criminal community. He is a cautious and clever lawyer who is always on his guard. However, Pip becomes friendly with Wemmick, the lawyer's clerk, and pays some pleasant visits to his quaint home in Walworth.

> **CHECKPOINT 2**
> Why does Dickens show us Jaggers at work?

During the next few years Pip learns how to spend money and gets into debt but he secretly arranges to help his friend Herbert in his career. His belief that he is being educated as a gentleman at Miss Havisham's expense so that he can marry Estella is strengthened when he is asked to accompany Estella in London. Estella tries to warn him that she has no feelings for him but he continues to hope.

Pip feels conscious that he has neglected Joe but he only goes to visit him to attend his sister's funeral. Joe's visit to Pip in London is an embarrassing occasion for them both.

One night Pip has a surprise visitor. It is the convict from the marshes, Abel Magwitch, who reveals that he is Pip's secret benefactor and he has returned illegally from Australia to see Pip. Pip is shocked, not least because this destroys his dream that he and Estella were destined to be married.

CHAPTERS 40–59: PIP AND MAGWITCH

Pip is horrified by the convict but feels bound to shelter him. He decides that, with Herbert's help, he will get Magwitch out of the

EXAMINER'S SECRET

All of the mysteries from parts one and two are resolved in the final part. Look at the way that Dickens keeps the reader waiting.

country. Pip learns that the convict Magwitch fought with on the marshes, and whom Magwitch blames for most of his troubles, is called Compeyson. This is the man who tricked Miss Havisham and failed to turn up to marry her.

Pip learns that Estella is to marry a surly, brutal man called Bentley Drummle, though he begs her not to throw herself away.

Wemmick warns Pip that he and Magwitch are being watched and the convict is lodged down the river, ready to catch a foreign steamer.

Gradually Pip pieces together the information that Magwitch is Estella's father and that her mother is Jaggers' servant, a woman he saved from the gallows. Estella was given to Miss Havisham as her adopted daughter.

After regretting her past mistakes and helping Pip to finance Herbert in business, Miss Havisham is burned and later dies from her injuries.

Pip is lured down to the marshes by Orlick, who admits he attacked Pip's sister and who almost succeeds in murdering Pip. Luckily, Herbert comes to the rescue.

As Pip and Magwitch attempt to catch a ship, they are caught by the police. In the struggle, the police informant, Compeyson, is drowned. Magwitch, who is injured, is tried and sentenced to death for returning to England. Magwitch dies before the sentence is carried out but not before Pip is able to tell him that his daughter is a beautiful lady and that he, Pip, loves her.

After Magwitch's death, Pip falls ill and is nursed by Joe. When he is well, he decides to go home and ask Biddy to marry him. He arrives to find it is Joe and Biddy's wedding day.

Pip accepts Herbert's offer of a job with his firm in Cairo. He returns after eleven years and accidentally meets Estella in the grounds of Satis House. She is now a widow. Pip feels sure that they will never part again.

DETAILED SUMMARIES

CHAPTERS 1–3 – Pip and the convict

1 Pip meets the convict in the graveyard.

2 There is a second convict out on the marshes.

3 Pip is frightened into keeping quiet about his strange meeting.

Pip is an orphan and is living with his sister, Mrs Joe Gargery. She has married a blacksmith and the three of them live on the Thames marshes. The marshes are bleak and largely uninhabited. His parents and his five brothers are buried in the local churchyard and Pip often visits their graves. It is on one such visit to the churchyard that Pip is surprised by the convict.

A large frightening man seizes hold of Pip, threatens with 'Keep still, you little devil, or I'll cut your throat' (Ch. 1, p. 4). He then turns Pip upside down in order to empty his pockets. The man has irons on his leg and is very nervous. When Pip says that his mother is nearby the convict panics and starts to run. Pip actually means that his mother is buried nearby. The convict learns that Pip lives with a blacksmith and demands a file, so that he can free his legs, and food, which he calls 'wittles' (Ch. 1, p. 5).

> **CHECKPOINT 3**
>
> Though frightening to Pip, the convict's actions can be seen as quite amusing. Why has Dickens done this?

> **GLOSSARY**
>
> **wittles** victuals, meaning food

The convict threatens Pip by telling him that he has a wicked young man with him who will find Pip and cut his liver out if he informs anyone about whom he has just seen. Though the convict is a powerfully built man, he does not hurt Pip.

Pip returns home to his sister and Joe. She has an exaggerated view of the role she has played in his upbringing and often makes remarks such as 'I've never had this apron of mine off, since born you were' (Ch. 2, p. 9). She is a fierce, violent woman who beats Pip and intimidates her husband. We are not given the name of Mrs Joe. This tends to make her a more distant character. Joe Gargery is a blacksmith, yet he is bullied by his wife. This adds humour to the story.

At the table, Pip hides his slice of bread in his trousers so that he can take it to the convict and keep his promise. The sound of large guns being fired makes Pip ask questions about the prison ships known as the hulks. The guns are fired when a prisoner escapes and Pip spends a restless night worrying that the young man is going to sneak into his bedroom and kill him.

Pip steals food from the pantry and sets off across the marshes to give it to the convict. The marshes take on a threatening appearance after Pip has met the convict. His experience has changed the way he sees the world around him. He comes upon a man dressed like the convict from the graveyard and with an iron on his leg.

Pip approaches the man from behind and is startled to find that this man is not the one to whom he is taking the food. The man tries to hit Pip but he manages to run away. At the old gun battery Pip meets the first convict and gives him the food. The convict is ravenous and eats the food so quickly that it astonishes Pip. When Pip says that he has seen the young man, the convict is amused that his story had been believed. When Pip goes on to describe him however, the convict becomes very anxious and says that he will 'pull him down, like a bloodhound' (Ch. 3, p. 21).

> **Two convicts**
> There is clearly a second escaped convict on the marshes. The first convict has some reason to want to hunt this man down. This helps to establish the plot of Magwitch and Compeyson.

CHAPTERS 4–6 – Christmas morning

1. **The Gargerys have visitors for Christmas lunch.**
2. **Soldiers arrive with news of the escaped convicts.**
3. **Pip joins in a hunt for the convicts.**
4. **The convicts are recaptured under odd circumstances.**

Pip explains his absence from the house on Christmas morning by saying that he has been to hear the carols. Joe and Pip go to church and Pip wants to tell someone what he has done. Pip has a strong sense of right and wrong and is troubled by not being able to own up to Joe. He would like to confess in church, but there is no opportunity as it is Christmas Day. Some visitors arrive for dinner: Mr Wopsle, the clerk at the church, Mr and Mrs Hubble and Uncle Pumblechook, Joe's uncle.

Uncle Pumblechook has brought a bottle of sherry and a bottle of port for Mrs Joe. This is a tradition, as is Mrs Joe's pretence that the house is always this cheerful. Mrs Joe becomes an even less sympathetic character in Chapter 4. She is mean and hypocritical. There is no mention of a Christmas present for Pip. He is barely allowed to be a child in Mrs Joe's house. At the end of the meal, Mrs Joe offers Pumblechook some brandy. Pip is terrified as he took some of the brandy to the convict and added water to the remainder. Pumblechook drinks the brandy and immediately runs out of the door and coughs and charges round. Pip had not added water to the brandy, but 'Tar-water' (Ch. 4, p. 29). There is nearly another calamity when Mrs Joe offers the guests some savoury pork pie; Pip had taken this to

CHECKPOINT 4
How does Dickens make it seem that Pip must be caught out?

CHECKPOINT 5
Why does Mrs Joe behave differently in front of the guests?

GLOSSARY
Tar-water a strong, black liquid made from pine bark

the convict, but he is saved by the arrival of a squad of soldiers who command everyone's attention.

CHECKPOINT 6

How do Pip's feelings influence the reader?

The sergeant is carrying handcuffs which Pip thinks are for him. This adds a touch of humour and shows his naivety. In fact, the handcuffs need repair and so the soldiers have come to the blacksmith. The sergeant announces that there are two escaped convicts on the marshes and that the soldiers expect to catch them at nightfall. Mr Pumblechook and the sergeant drink the wine that was supposed to be for Mrs Joe, then the soldiers leave to look for the escaped prisoners. Pip, Joe and Mr Wopsle accompany them. They follow the sound of shouting until they find two men fighting in a ditch. One is clearly stopping the other from running away, even though this means that both men will be caught. The man Pip describes as 'my convict' (Ch. 5, p. 37) says of the other man 'Do you see what a villain he is?' (Ch. 5, p. 37) and is pleased that this villain has been recaptured. He also says that he stole a pie and some other food from the blacksmith's house, thus preventing suspicion from falling on Pip.

EXAMINER'S SECRET

A sign of a good candidate is the ability to cross-reference, e.g. provide evidence of the conflict between the two convicts from different parts of the novel.

Pip's conscience bothers him, but he still does not tell Joe what has happened.

> ### Sewing the seed
>
> The link between the two convicts is very strong, but unexplained. This hints at the reappearance of this plot strand later in the novel.

CHAPTERS 7–8 – Miss Havisham

❶ Pip is to be Joe's apprentice.

❷ Pip meets Miss Havisham and Estella.

❸ Miss Havisham is strangely dressed in a faded old bridal gown.

Twelve months have passed since the episode with the convicts. Pip is to be apprenticed to Joe when he is old enough. He attends an evening school in the village, run by Mr Wopsle's great-aunt. She sleeps through the lessons and Pip has largely to teach himself to read, write and do simple sums. He writes a letter, in very basic English, to Joe. Learning to read and write does not come easily to Pip, and he receives no help from home. Pip is proud of the letter and Joe is delighted with it, though the only part he can read is his own first name. This leads to Joe telling Pip of his own difficult childhood with a drunken father who beat Joe and his mother. It is because of this experience that Joe is so tolerant of his wife. He does not want to find himself behaving like his own father has done. Joe does not condemn his father for the years of brutality, but insists that the man had a good 'hart' (Ch. 7, p. 46). This shows Joe to be a very tolerant and forgiving man. Pip admires Joe for this and finds himself looking up to the blacksmith from this point onwards.

Mrs Joe arrives back from market where she has been assisting Pumblechook. She announces that the rich, reclusive Miss Havisham has asked for Pip to go and play at her house. Pumblechook suggested him to Miss Havisham when she was making enquiries to find a boy who would go and play there. Pip is scrubbed down and sent off with Pumblechook who is to take him to Miss Havisham the following morning. Pip has not actually been asked whether he would like to go to Miss Havisham's at all.

Pip is taken to the run-down house of Miss Havisham and meets Estella for the first time. Pumblechook is peeved that he is not invited into the house with Pip. Estella tells Pip that the house is called 'Satis', meaning enough. She leads him by candlelight to the room in which Miss Havisham sits. Miss Havisham is dressed as a bride but everything in the room has aged and faded, including her. All watches and clocks in the room are stopped at twenty minutes to nine.

Miss Havisham tells Pip 'I have a sick fancy that I want to see some play' (Ch. 8, p. 59). When Pip finds this difficult to do in such gloomy surroundings, Estella is sent for. She plays cards with Pip and humiliates him repeatedly, commenting that he is common as 'He calls the knaves, Jacks, this boy' (Ch. 8, p. 60). Pip is told to come back in six days time and gets to explore some of the grounds of the house before Estella shows him out. She is happy that she is able to make

> **CHECKPOINT 7**
>
> How does Dickens introduce mystery around Miss Havisham?

> **CHECKPOINT 8**
>
> Estella is cruel, but she is also lonely herself. Who might have affected her character?

EXAMINER'S SECRET
Dickens is deliberately vague about Miss Havisham's past. This allows him later to introduce the idea that she might be Pip's benefactor.

him cry and Pip feels ignorant and resents his simple upbringing. Pip is captivated by Estella's beauty but does not know how to handle the cruelty she shows him.

A new story

A new storyline, focused on Miss Havisham and Estella, is now developed. Miss Havisham is a pathetic character who has withdrawn from the world. Why she is withdrawn and how this is related to the subplot concerning the convicts is left unanswered.

CHAPTERS 9–10 – The two pound notes

1 **Pip is given two pounds by a sinister stranger.**

2 **The stranger clearly knows Pip's convict.**

Pip is concerned that if he says what Miss Havisham and Satis House are really like, people will form the wrong impression. He is bullied by Mrs Joe and Pumblechook and so decides to invent an elaborate story about his visit. He says that:

- Miss Havisham is very tall and dark
- She was sitting in a black velvet coach
- Estella handed in wine and cake from a golden plate
- Four huge dogs ate veal cutlets from a silver basket
- They had all played with flags and swords
- There was a cupboard containing swords, pistols, jam and pills

Pip feels protective towards Miss Havisham and Estella, even though they are quite harsh with him. His list of items in the cupboard is ridiculous and shows that his imagination is running away with him. Pip is happy to lie to Mrs Joe and Pumblechook, but has to tell the truth to Joe. Later, Pip admits to Joe that he had been lying and Joe scolds him, but reassures the boy that he is not ignorant and backward, as Estella had said, but a great scholar.

Pip asks Biddy if she will teach him when he goes to the evening school and she agrees. On the way home, Pip calls at the Three Jolly Bargemen to collect Joe. There is a stranger in the pub who takes an interest in Pip. He appears to know about the episode with the convict on the marshes and reveals this to Pip by stirring his drink 'not with a spoon that was brought to him, but with a file' (Ch. 10, p. 77). It was the same file that Pip had given to the convict a year earlier. The stranger gives Pip some money, which turns out to be the grand sum of two pounds. The mysterious stranger and his gift must have some significance. Pip feels that there is a link with his convict. When he gets home and realises he has been given so much, Pip tries to return the money. When he returns to the Three Jolly Bargemen, the man has gone. The two pound notes are wrapped up and kept safe.

> ### CHECKPOINT 9
> How has Pip been affected by Estella?

The distance begins

Instead of rejecting the strangers at Satis House, Pip shows an affinity for them and is happy to distance himself from those who have bullied him for most of his life.

CHAPTER 11 – Herbert Pocket and the stranger on the stairs

❶ Pip meets Miss Havisham's relatives.

❷ Mr Jaggers makes his first appearance.

❸ There is a man in Miss Havisham's past.

Pip makes his second visit to Satis House. Estella shows him to a different part of the house where he is made to wait in a room which already has people in it – Sarah Pocket, Camilla and her husband, cousin Raymond, and Georgiana.

They are talking about someone called Tom and someone called Matthew, whose behaviour they do not approve of. Estella knows these people and the intrigue behind their visit. She leads Pip to Miss Havisham's room and taunts him on the way. She makes Pip say that she is pretty and then insults him. Estella is vain and is encouraged in this by Miss Havisham. She is also lonely and used to amusing herself

CHECKPOINT 10

Why is this man's striking physical appearance described so carefully?

A burly man passes Pip on the stairs. 'His eyes are set very deep in his head, and were disagreeably sharp and suspicious' (Ch. 11, p. 83). Pip reveals that this man is to be important to him later on. Miss Havisham leads Pip into a different room from that of his first visit. It is a large room with a very long table in it. On the table are the remnants of a wedding cake on an 'epergne' (Ch. 11, p. 84), covered in cobwebs and infested with spiders. The room has decayed as much as has Miss Havisham and she affects the whole environment of the house. Pip is made to walk Miss Havisham round the room and then to call for Estella. She arrives with the four visitors who take it in turn to flatter Miss Havisham. The visitors attempt to outdo one another in their efforts to impress Miss Havisham:

- Sarah Pocket says Miss Havisham looks well

- Camilla complains of her infirmities and says she lies awake at night thinking of Miss Havisham

- Raymond adds that his wife's worries about family troubles are making one of her legs shorter than the other

- Georgiana tries to be the last to say goodbye to Miss Havisham but is beaten in this by Sarah Pocket

They discuss Matthew again. Apparently he refuses to visit. Miss Havisham is sure that he will come to see her when she is dead and laid out on the long table. The visitors have come to see Miss Havisham because it is her birthday. She does not celebrate it and does not even want it to be mentioned. Miss Havisham talks of her death and says it 'will be the finished curse upon him' (Ch. 11, p. 89) though she does not explain who this 'he' actually is. Miss Havisham was to have been married on her birthday. The coincidence of these two supposedly happy days creates more **pathos** when we see what she has become. Pip is then made to play cards with Estella, who treats him with scorn, though she does not actually insult him this time.

Pip explores the run-down grounds of the house and meets a boy of his own age (Herbert Pocket) who insists that they should fight. A boxing match takes place and Pip easily beats the other boy, who keeps on fighting until he has been almost knocked out. Estella seems to have been watching and she appears to be pleased with Pip, so much so that she lets him kiss her on the cheek as he leaves.

CHECKPOINT 11

Why do the visitors not dare to contradict their host, even when this makes them look foolish?

? DID YOU KNOW?

Dickens is being ironic in calling Miss Havisham's house 'Satis'. There can be no satisfaction there for Miss Havisham, Estella or Pip.

GLOSSARY

epergne a fancy cake stand

Another new element

Charles Dickens introduces a new element to the plot, the Pocket family, and links it to the strange behaviour of Miss Havisham. This develops intrigue.

CHAPTERS 12–14 – Joe and Pip

① Miss Havisham plans for Pip to become Joe's apprentice.

② Miss Havisham seems to enjoy Estella upsetting Pip.

③ Joe visits Satis House.

④ Pip is sworn in as Joe's apprentice.

CHECKPOINT 12

Even though Miss Havisham helps Pip, she allows Estella to behave badly. Why is this?

Pip is worried about having hurt the boy with whom he fought at Miss Havisham's. He returns nervously to the house and pushes Miss Havisham in her chair. He continues to call every other day at noon for eight to ten months. Miss Havisham asks him what he is going to be and Pip tells her of the plans for him to be apprenticed to Joe.

Estella continues to treat Pip with disdain, though sometimes she is quite friendly towards him which confuses him. Miss Havisham seems to take great delight in Estella's ability to captivate Pip and urges her to 'break their hearts and have no mercy!' (Ch. 12, p. 95). Estella is beautiful but cruel. She has been heavily influenced by the bitterness of Miss Havisham towards men.

Pumblechook insists on interfering in the plans for Pip's future and the boy becomes increasingly infuriated with him. Miss Havisham asks Pip to bring Joe to see her so that the matter of Pip's apprenticeship can be settled. Mrs Joe is incensed at the invitation to Joe as it excludes her.

Joe and Pip visit Satis House and are shown in by Estella, who takes no notice of either of them. Throughout the conversation with Miss Havisham, Joe addresses Pip instead of her. This makes Pip feel ashamed of Joe. However, the absurd conversation between Joe and Miss Havisham is typical of the way Charles Dickens creates humour through eccentric behaviour. Miss Havisham gives the blacksmith twenty-five guineas to pay for Pip to be apprenticed to him and she makes Joe agree that he will not look for any more money from her. Joe does not seem to realise the difference between pounds and guineas, possibly because he has never had so much money in his life before. Miss Havisham does not need to make Joe promise not to seek anything else from her. She is being rather mean and suspicious. Pip is told that he is not to visit again.

Joe hands over the money to his wife and Pip is taken to the Town Hall to have his 'indentures' (Ch. 13, p. 105) sworn out. A party is held in Pip's honour, but by the end of it he feels that he will never settle to Joe's trade, even though he once dreamt of being a blacksmith.

Pip is not satisfied with his trade but he does not complain as he does not want to upset Joe. He thinks of Estella a great deal and wishes that he could see her again.

Marriage

There are many examples of unhappy marriages in Charles Dickens' work. In *Great Expectations* he explores this theme of failed marriage and unhappy family life in great depth.

Note that:

- Miss Havisham was badly treated regarding marriage.
- Estella has been brought up to be used as a weapon against men.
- Pip cannot bring himself to accept Biddy.
- Biddy's marriage to Joe is hardly ideal.
- Mr Jaggers has never married.
- Herbert worries about providing for Clara.
- Magwitch never gets to see his daughter.
- Estella's mother lives a miserable life.
- Wemmick's make-believe world has the only happy marriage of the novel.

EXAMINER'S SECRET

It is always a good idea to collect a range of words to describe a character.

CHECKPOINT 13

How are Pip's feelings towards Joe changing?

DID YOU KNOW?

Miss Havisham pays Joe in guineas, which went out of circulation in 1817. They were still legal tender but show Miss Havisham's old-fashioned ways.

GLOSSARY

indentures a formal contract binding Pip to Joe as his apprentice

CHAPTER 15 – Orlick causes trouble

1 Orlick resents Pip's presence in the forge.

2 Joe fights with Orlick and humiliates him.

3 Pip finds that Estella has gone abroad.

4 Mrs Joe is attacked.

Pip continues his education under Biddy and Wopsle, but neither teaches him very much. Wopsle uses Pip as an audience for his eccentric performances and sermons. Pip feels that he should visit Miss Havisham (and Estella) again, but Joe feels that she will think the boy wants something from her.

CHECKPOINT 14

Think why Orlick is described in an unsympathetic way. (He is constantly referred to as 'slouching'.)

Joe's 'journeyman' (p. 112) assistant Orlick is introduced. He is a bad-tempered man and resents Pip's appearance in the forge. He says that his first name is Dolge, but Pip thinks this unlikely. When Pip asks for a half-holiday, Orlick insists that he should have one too. Joe agrees, but his wife scolds him for being weak. This leads to an argument between Orlick and Mrs Joe. He calls her 'a foul shrew, Mother Gargery' (p. 114) and Joe has to intervene. Joe and Orlick fight; Joe wins easily. An uneasy peace descends on the forge.

Pip visits Satis House where Sarah Pocket admits him reluctantly. Miss Havisham tells Pip that Estella is abroad, being educated. She takes a wicked satisfaction from the fact that this news upsets Pip. Miss Havisham is very cruel to Pip, even though his visit is purely out of friendship.

On the way home, Pip meets Wopsle and is persuaded to join him and Pumblechook in reading 'the affecting tragedy of George Barnwell' (p. 117). They spend several hours doing this and when they head home they come across Orlick who is waiting beside the road. Keeping Pip at Pumblechook's allows Charles Dickens to have the attack on Mrs Joe take place without the boy's knowledge. He says that he has been up town and was not far behind the others. He points out that the guns at the Hulks are firing again, showing that a prisoner has escaped. When they pass the Three Jolly Bargemen they hear that someone has entered the house when Joe was out and that a person has been attacked. They run to the house and Pip finds his sister unconscious; she has been 'knocked down by a tremendous blow on the back of her head, dealt by some unkown hand' (p. 119). The argument and the fight should put Orlick under suspicion for the attack on Mrs Joe. Notice that it is Orlick who mentions the guns firing from the Hulks. An escaped convict is good cover for an attack.

A set-up

The attack on Mrs Joe marks a definite stage in Pip's life. From this point onward there is little to hold Pip back.

The final part of the novel is also set up here as the reader knows that Orlick bears a grudge against Pip and the he is capable of being violent. The malice of Orlick means that there is no further explanation needed for his actions later in the novel.

CHAPTERS 16–17 – Mrs Joe fails to recover

1 A leg-iron is found next to Mrs Joe.

2 Mrs Joe never recovers from her injuries.

3 Pip suspects Orlick.

The events surrounding the attack on Pip's sister are explained:

- Before nine o'clock, a farm labourer had seen her in the doorway of the kitchen. Joe was in the Three Jolly Bargemen at the time.

- When Joe returned home at five to ten he found his wife on the floor.

- The fire had not burnt down, but the candle had been blown out.

- Mrs Joe had been struck with something heavy on the head and the spine and then something heavy had been thrown down at her.

CHECKPOINT 15

Why is it important that suspicion should fall on Orlick?

GLOSSARY

journeyman a skilled or semi-skilled worker who worked for a skilled tradesman

the tragedy of George Barnwell a popular play from the eighteenth century. Barnwell is persuaded by his lover to rob his master and kill his uncle. He and his lover are hanged.

CHECK THE BOOK

Look Back in Anger (1956) is a play by John Osborne in which a young man struggles to come to terms with his role in society and with the problems of social class.

- On the ground beside her was found a convict's leg-iron which had been filed open. Joe announces that it has not been filed open recently. Pip is sure that it is his convict's iron, the one he supplied the file for. He is frightened.

Though Mrs Joe has never got on with Orlick, it is him she sends for after she has been injured. Pip suspects Orlick but he has made sure that he has been seen in town during the evening. The constables and the 'Bow Street Men' (Ch. 16, p. 122) stay around the house for two weeks, accuse numerous innocent people and then leave. The culprit i not caught.

Mrs Joe never recovers from her injuries. She is left unable to speak and seems to understand little of what is said to her. Biddy joins the household on the death of her previous employer. Mrs Joe traces out what appears to be a capital letter T, which puzzles everyone. Pip eventually thinks it may be a drawing of a hammer and Biddy realises that it is meant to represent Orlick. She develops a fondness for Pip's company, which puzzles him.

Pip carries on his apprenticeship and visits Miss Havisham on his birthday. Pip observes that Satis House has not changed since the first time he visited it. Pip notices that Biddy is growing into an attractive woman, but he is still preoccupied with Estella. Pip is still trying to learn to read and write, but Biddy picks up things much more quickly than he does. Pip confesses that 'I want to be a gentleman' (Ch. 17, p. 127) and wishes to lead a very different life. This disappoints Biddy. He tells her that he could not hope to win Estella if he were to remain common. He says that he wishes he could fall in love with Biddy but she tells him that he never will. Orlick has been paying Biddy some attention, but she hates him as much as Pip does.

Biddy shows her maturity

Pip is insensitive in the way in which he speaks to Biddy about Estella. Biddy would clearly like Pip to fall in love with her, but realises that he would never be satisfied. Dickens lets the reader know that Pip is immature and selfish through his treatment of Biddy.

CHAPTERS 18–19 – Mr Jaggers and Pip's education

1 Jaggers tells Pip of the young man's new fortune.

2 Pip has a mysterious benefactor.

3 Pip assumes that Miss Havisham is responsible for his new wealth.

4 Pip leaves for London.

Pip is in the fourth year of his apprenticeship. Wopsle is reading an account of a gruesome murder to a group of friends at the Three Jolly Bargemen. Pip and Joe are present. Wopsle is just about to declare that the accused is clearly guilty when he is interrupted by a stranger. This stranger is recognised by Pip as being the man who passed him on the stairs of Satis House. The man questions Wopsle's knowledge of the law and shows him up. He then asks to speak privately to Joe and Pip, whom he has been sent to seek out.

The stranger introduces himself as Mr Jaggers, a lawyer from London. He tells Pip that the boy has great expectations and 'will come into a handsome property' (Ch. 18, p. 138). The boy is told he must begin his education as a gentleman at once. Pip and Joe are astonished; Joe agrees to release the boy from his indentures. Jaggers says that there is one condition attached to the fortune that Pip is to inherit; he is not allowed to know the name of the person who is his benefactor. Pip is not even allowed to make the least enquiry as to his benefactor's identity. The boy is to keep the name of Pip. Mr Jaggers shows that he is a very just man and impresses Pip with his integrity. Because Miss Haversham knows Jaggers, Pip is sure that she is responsible for his great expectations.

Jaggers says that Pip must begin his education in London and that Matthew Pocket could be enlisted as a tutor. Pip recognises Matthew as the person who Miss Havisham thought would visit when she came to be laid out on the long table, dead. The suggestion of Matthew Pocket as Pip's tutor intrigues him, possibly as he thinks Matthew might shed some light on the situation with Miss Havisham. Joe tells Biddy that 'Pip's a gentleman of fortun' then' (Ch. 18, p. 143). Pip is impatient to leave for London to begin his new life.

> **.CHECKPOINT 17**
>
> What conclusion does Pip jump to regarding Miss Havisham?

> **GLOSSARY**
>
> **Bow Street Men** policemen from the main London police station in Bow Street

Pip tells Biddy he would like Joe to visit him in London, but that he is worried Joe might seem out of place. Biddy sharply points out that Joe is proud and would not want to be made a fool of. Pip handles the situation badly. He is already beginning to see himself as superior. Pip feels no shame over this, in fact he enjoys it. Pip is so wrapped up in himself that he never stops to consider the feelings of Joe or Biddy.

Pip visits Mr Trabb, the tailor, who fawns after the boy when he hears of his new wealth. Trabb's boy is humiliated by being made to run about after Pip who had been his equal until recently.

Pip visits Pumblechook, who tries to take credit for setting Pip off on the road that led to his fortune. Pumblechook also assumes that Miss Havisham is Pip's mysterious benefactor. Pumblechook gives Pip fine food and wine and speaks to him like an old friend. He then suggests that Pip might like to invest in his corn business. Compare this to the way Pumblechook used to speak to Pip when Mrs Joe was present.

On the final day, Pip dresses in his new suit and visits Satis House. Sarah Pocket admits him and he visits Miss Havisham as she is taking another of her walks around her candlelit room. He tells Miss Havisham of his good fortune and says he is grateful for it. She has already heard from Mr Jaggers and she questions Pip as to the name of the rich person who has adopted him. Miss Havisham tells him to 'Be good – deserve it – and abide by Mr Jaggers' instructions' (Ch. 19, p. 158). She finally comments that he will always keep the name of Pip. Pip does not see that Miss Havisham's recent treatment of him is totally at odds with her providing him with a fortune. He takes the handsome property to mean Satis House. Pip thinks that Miss Havisham's questions are a trap and they confirm for him that she is his benefactor. Her final comment about his name reinforces this idea.

Pip says goodbye to Joe and Biddy and takes the coach to London. Only then does he begin to think he might have behaved ungratefully to Joe.

> **CHECKPOINT 18**
>
> How is Pip's immaturity revealed in the conversation with Miss Havisham?

 Now take a break!

WHO SAYS ...?

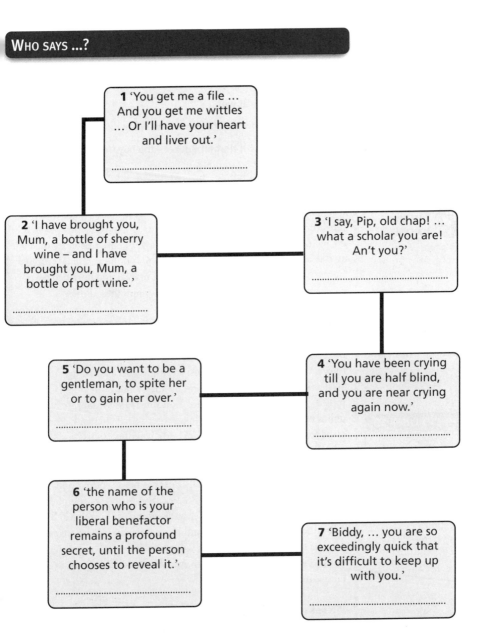

1 'You get me a file … And you get me wittles … Or I'll have your heart and liver out.'

....

2 'I have brought you, Mum, a bottle of sherry wine – and I have brought you, Mum, a bottle of port wine.'

....

3 'I say, Pip, old chap! … what a scholar you are! An't you?'

....

4 'You have been crying till you are half blind, and you are near crying again now.'

....

5 'Do you want to be a gentleman, to spite her or to gain her over.'

....

6 'the name of the person who is your liberal benefactor remains a profound secret, until the person chooses to reveal it.'

....

7 'Biddy, … you are so exceedingly quick that it's difficult to keep up with you.'

....

Check your answers on p. 89.

CHAPTERS 20–2 – Pip and Herbert in London

❶ Pip arrives in London.

❷ We see Jaggers at work.

❸ Miss Havisham was jilted on her wedding day.

❹ Pip meets up with Herbert Pocket – the boy from the boxing match.

After a journey of five hours Pip arrives in London. He is impressed by its size and ugliness. A hackney coachman takes him to Mr Jaggers' office where a clerk tells him that the lawyer is in court. Pip is shown into Mr Jaggers' room to wait but he finds it 'a most dismal place' (Ch. 20, p. 164), particularly as it contains two very ugly plaster casts of swollen faces. He decides to take a walk round the area and is disgusted by the blood and dirt of Smithfield meat market and horrified by the gatekeeper of Newgate prison who shows him the gallows.

Back at Jaggers' he finds that several other people are awaiting the lawyer's return. These turn out to be clients and Jaggers deals with them in a firm and sometimes brutal manner when he arrives. He rejects one client's bogus witness in disgust because of his appearance: 'ask him what he means by bringing such a fellow as that' (Ch. 20, p. 170). Pip's first impressions of London are very depressing – ugliness, dirt, the gallows and Jaggers' criminal clients. Jaggers inspires great fear and respect in his clients. He is willing to use tricks like false witnesses but he is careful to keep himself in the clear.

When they are alone Jaggers tells Pip that he is sending him to stay at Barnard's Inn with young Mr Pocket until Monday when he will be taken to visit Mr Pocket's father to see if it suits him there. Mr Jaggers tells him about his allowance and the arrangements for credit with various tradesmen. He says he will try to keep Pip out of debt but no doubt Pip will go wrong somehow. The clerk, Wemmick, is told to take Pip to Barnard's Inn.

Pip talks to Wemmick on the way and thinks him to be a rather dry little man in appearance and manner. Wemmick is surprised when Pip offers to shake his hand on parting. He says he has got out of the habit.

DID YOU KNOW?

Pip's first impressions of London are coloured by the gallows and the criminal law business. Dickens includes his own views on British law.

CHECKPOINT 19

What does Jaggers' behaviour tell you about the law?

Barnard's Inn is a shabby collection of buildings in a poor state of repair. Mr Pocket Junior's rooms are on the top floor and Pip finds a note saying that the occupant is out but will be back shortly. Pip is surprised when the young man appears because he recognises him as the boy he fought with at Miss Havisham's house. Eventually, after showing Pip round and trying to make him feel at home, the young man recognises him.

Pip and the young man both burst out laughing at the coincidence. The young man is Herbert Pocket and says there were hopes that Miss Havisham might have favoured him and settled some fortune on him, but she did not. He tells Pip that Estella was adopted by Miss Havisham and has been brought up to exact revenge on the male sex. He also says that Mr Jaggers is Miss Havisham's man of business.

Pip takes an immediate liking to Herbert who strikes him as open, generous and cheerful. Pip confides in him and tells him all about his upbringing at the smithy. He asks Herbert to put him straight about manners and during their meal, the conversation is regularly interrupted as Herbert gently corrects Pip in his handling of the cutlery and his eating habits. Herbert gives Pip the name Handel, after the composer who wrote 'The Harmonious Blacksmith'.

Pip learns that many years before, Miss Havisham had been jilted on her wedding day, 'At that hour and minute … at which she afterwards stopped all the clocks' (Ch. 22, p. 182). She had let the house go to ruin and had not seen daylight since.

During the weekend Herbert shows Pip around London and on the Monday he takes him to his parents' house at Hammersmith. Mrs Pocket is a disorganised woman with seven young children and two nursemaids who seem to be constantly tripping over. Mr Pocket senior comes out to meet Pip.

DID YOU KNOW?

Dickens uses Herbert as a narrator to fill in the gaps in the plot.

More proof?

The belief that Miss Havisham is his benefactor seems to be confirmed by the connection between her and Jaggers. Herbert seems to be of the same opinion.

CHAPTERS 23–5 – Pip enjoys life with the Pockets

❶ **Pip meets Bentley Drummle.**

❷ **Wemmick shows Pip round his extraordinary house.**

The Pocket household appears to be run by and for the servants. Mrs Pocket takes little notice of what goes on around her. She is greatly concerned with the fact that her father was nearly a member of the nobility. Mr Pocket, who is to be Pip's tutor, is a pleasant man whose patience is severely tested by the disorder in the household. He welcomes Pip and shows him to his room. He has two other boarding pupils, Startop and Bentley Drummle. The evening meal is a chaotic affair disrupted by incidents involving the children and servants.

Pip settles in at the Pocket house but feels he would like to keep his room at Barnard's Inn and so be able to share his time between the two. He goes to see Mr Jaggers who provides him with money to buy furniture. Pip finds that Jaggers' way of dealing with him makes him uncomfortable but Wemmick reassures him that 'it's not personal; it's professional: only professional' (Ch. 24, p. 198).

Wemmick shows Pip round the premises and tells him that the two ugly plaster casts are death masks of ex-clients taken after they were hanged.

Wemmick invites Pip to visit his home at Walworth at some future date. He asks if Jaggers has invited Pip to dine with him yet and suggests that when he does Pip should take a look at his housekeeper. At Wemmick's suggestion they go to a police court to watch Mr Jaggers at work. Pip gets the impression that everyone there is terrified of Jaggers, even the magistrates. Pip does not know how to deal with Jaggers but comes to realise that he has a formidable reputation in the criminal world.

At Hammersmith, Pip enjoys rowing on the river with Herbert and the other two pupils. He finds Drummle surly and proud and prefers the company of the more gentle Startop. Pip's education proceeds well but he is also learning how to spend money. We are seeing the beginnings of Pip's extravagance with money.

CHECKPOINT 20

What purpose does the visit to Wemmick's house serve?

After a few weeks Pip writes to Wemmick and arranges to go home with him to Walworth one evening. They meet at Jaggers' office and make the journey on foot. When they reach Wemmick's house Pip is surprised to find that it is a little wooden building like a toy castle, complete with drawbridge, flagpole and a small cannon. Wemmick proudly informs Pip that this is all his own work. He asks Pip not to mention his home life to Jaggers as he likes to keep the office and the Castle separate.

Inside, Pip is introduced to Wemmick's elderly father who is extremely deaf. Pip is encouraged to please the old man by nodding his head frequently. At nine o'clock Wemmick goes out and fires the cannon, which delights his father, as it is the only sound he can hear. Pip stays the night and in the morning walks to Jaggers' office with Wemmick, noticing that Wemmick's manner becomes more stiff and hard the nearer he gets to his place of work. The visit to Wemmick's home is a comic but touching episode. We see that Wemmick is a kindly and sensitive man when he is away from his depressing working environment.

Wemmick's world

Wemmick's make-believe world is in stark contrast to the harsh reality of life in London. Notice how Wemmick becomes a completely different character when he is away from the oppressive atmosphere of Mr Jaggers' office.

This is a rare example of a happy home life in the novel.

CHECKPOINT 21

How does Wemmick change when he is at home?

 CHECK THE FILM

David Lean's film of *Oliver Twist* (1948) – another Charles Dickens novel – gives a good insight into the life of the criminal underclass in London.

CHAPTERS 26–8 – Dinner with Jaggers

❶ Pip and his friends dine with Jaggers.

❷ Jaggers has a frightening housekeeper.

Jaggers invites Pip to dine with him the following evening and tells him to bring Herbert, Drummle and Startop. They all meet at the lawyer's office and Jaggers conducts them to his house in Soho which Pip finds to be a grim, dark building. Jaggers examines Pip's companions and at once takes a great interest in Drummle who he names 'the Spider' (Ch. 26, p. 212) because he is 'The blotchy, sprawly, sulky fellow' (Ch. 26, p. 212). Pip feels that Jaggers has a talent for discovering the worst sides of people's characters. Pip takes the opportunity to observe Jaggers' housekeeper whom Wemmick had described as 'a wild beast tamed' (Ch. 24, p. 202). She is a tall pale woman of about forty. She seems tense and always keeps her eyes on Jaggers.

> **CHECKPOINT 22**
>
> Why might Jaggers seem fascinated by the surly Drummle and christen him 'the spider'?

After Drummle has been boasting about his strength Jaggers makes his housekeeper show her wrists, much against her will. He tells them he has never known a stronger grip in man or woman. Drummle becomes increasingly rude and unpleasant. Jaggers appears to enjoy this but he eventually has to stop him from throwing a glass at Startop. Later he tells Pip that he likes 'the Spider' but that Pip should stay clear of him. About a month later, Drummle finishes his tuition at Mr Pocket's and goes home.

Pip receives a letter from Biddy to say that Joe is coming to London with Mr Wopsle and would like to visit him. This is not welcome news as Pip has become ashamed of his background. Joe's visit is embarrassing and awkward as the blacksmith feels completely out of place. He is clumsy and confused and upsets Pip by calling him 'sir' (Ch. 27, p. 220). Pip has become a snob and has begun to deceive himself. Even though Joe's discomfort is comical, his simple dignity is a reproach to Pip. Joe delivers a message from Miss Havisham that Estella has come home and would like to see Pip. Joe refuses Pip's invitation to dinner and suggests that Pip would see him in a better light if he visited him at the forge.

The next day Pip sets out for home. At first he intends to stay with Joe and Biddy at the forge but he manages to convince himself that this would be an inconvenience to them and that he ought to stay at the Blue Boar. Two convicts are on the coach. They are being taken down to the prison ships off the marshes and Pip is horrified when he recognises one of them as the man who gave him two pound notes in the Three Jolly Bargemen one Saturday night. The convict does not recognise Pip but Pip overhears him telling his companion how another convict had asked him to give the two pounds to a boy who had fed him and kept his secret. Pip gets off the coach as soon as it reaches town and goes to the Blue Boar. Pip seems to be haunted by his background. The convict on the coach makes him realise how easily he could be exposed.

> **DID YOU KNOW?**
>
> Victorian prisons were overcrowded and ships were regularly used to house prisoners.

Linking the threads

Pip has an unpleasant reminder of the convict on the marshes. This reminds the reader of this part of the plot, ready for the appearance of Magwitch.

CHAPTERS 29–31 – Pip and Estella at Satis House

1. Pip meets Estella again.
2. Jaggers has Orlick dismissed because of Pip's unease.
3. Herbert warns Pip about Estella.
4. Mr Wopsle performs *Hamlet*.

In the morning, Pip goes to Miss Havisham's house and is unpleasantly surprised to find that Orlick is employed there as gatekeeper. Sarah Pocket is also at the house. When Pip goes into Miss Havisham's room he does not immediately recognise the elegant lady who is sitting next to her. When she looks at him he realises that it is Estella and he finds her more beautiful than ever.

Miss Havisham encourages them to walk in the garden together and they talk of old times. Pip is puzzled by something that he sees in Estella but he cannot work out what it is. Estella warns Pip that she has no heart, no softness or sentiment but Pip is still convinced that Miss Havisham intends that they should be married. This is only strengthened later when Miss Havisham puts her arm round his neck and fiercely urges him to love Estella.

Mr Jaggers arrives and both he and Pip are surprised to see each other. At dinner Jaggers is very quiet and avoids looking at Estella. It is arranged that Pip will meet Estella at the coach when she travels to London. Pip returns to the Blue Boar and thinks of Estella. He has not gone to visit Joe as he imagines Estella would not approve of him keeping up such lowly connections.

Next day Pip tells Jaggers of his misgivings about Orlick and Jaggers says he will sack him. Pip walks part of the way out of town so as to avoid meeting Pumblechook who has been telling everyone he is responsible for Pip's good fortune. He is mocked by the tailor's boy and is glad to get away and into the coach.

Back at Barnard's Inn, Pip tells Herbert about his love for Estella but Herbert knows saying, 'You have always adored her, ever since I have known you' (Ch. 30, p. 247). He, too, is of the opinion that Miss Havisham is Pip's benefactor, but he tries to warn Pip that attachment to Estella may bring him unhappiness. He reminds Pip about her upbringing. Herbert confides to Pip that he is secretly engaged to a young woman called Clara who lives with her invalid father. He fears that his mother would not approve of the girl's social position and he is not yet in a position to marry and support a wife. Herbert is a deliberate contrast to Pip, Herbert is in love with a girl of humble circumstances. Pip finds a playbill which Joe had given him. It advertises a performance of *Hamlet* starring Mr Wopsle and the two friends decide to go to it.

The performance of the play is incompetent and ridiculous. The actors are frequently interrupted and insulted by members of the audience. Mr Wopsle in the leading role is a particular victim of their low humour. Pip finds himself laughing despite feeling sorry for Wopsle. The friends try to leave quietly but are unable to avoid being taken to speak to the star who now calls himself Waldengarver. They are as polite about the play as they can be and out of pity they invite him home for supper. The description of the play in its detail and in the behaviour of the audience is a wonderful piece of comic writing.

> **CHECKPOINT 24**
>
> What does the visit to the play bring to the novel?

CHAPTERS 32–5 – Back at the forge

1 Pip meets Estella and still loves her.

2 Mrs Joe has died.

3 Pip is still wary of Orlick.

One day Pip receives a message from Estella. She is arriving in London the following day and requests Pip to meet her. Pip is at the coach office several hours early and while he is waiting he happens to meet Wemmick who is on his way to Newgate prison and he offers to show Pip round. Pip accepts and accompanies the clerk as he visits several of Jaggers' clients. After the visit he feels contaminated by the awful place and he walks around the area to free himself from its influence before meeting Estella.

When she arrives Estella seems more beautiful than ever. She behaves towards Pip with a strange mixture of friendliness and formality and reminds him that they are not free to do as they please. Pip is to take her to Richmond where she is to stay with a lady who is to introduce her into fashionable society. When she gives Pip her hand and he kisses it she reminds him of her warning about her lack of feeling but she allows him to kiss her cheek. Pip feels his love is hopeless but he cannot help himself. He still believes that there is a plan that he and Estella shall marry although he is hurt by her manner towards him. He still disregards her warnings.

> **CHECKPOINT 25**
>
> Why is Pip haunted by a sense of there being some strange connection between Estella and Jaggers?

On the way to Richmond they talk about Mr Jaggers and Pip experiences 'that inexplicable feeling I had had before' (Ch. 33, p. 269). Pip delivers Estella to Richmond and returns to the Pockets' house in Hammersmith.

Good fortune has not brought Pip happiness although he tries to convince himself he is having a good time. He is troubled about his neglectful behaviour towards Joe and Biddy and he feels he has been leading Herbert into extravagance and debt. They have applied to join a drinking and dining club, of which Bentley Drummle is a member, and begin to keep late nights in an empty pursuit of pleasure. At times the two friends make futile attempts to organise their finances. One evening, after going over the bills, Pip receives a letter with a black border which informs him that his sister has died and that her funeral will take place on the following Monday.

Pip believes that Orlick was responsible for his sister's injuries and is filled with anger but he knows he has no proof. The funeral is a grim farce organised by Trabb & Co. with professional mourners and lots of black crepe. Pumblechook and the Hubbles are in attendance. Joe says he would have preferred a more simple and homely burial but he thinks that this way shows more respect. In his description of the funeral, Dickens shows us his skill in creating humour in tragic circumstances.

After the funeral Pip dines with Joe and Biddy at the forge and asks if he may stay the night in his old room. When he stays the night at the forge Pip has a sense that he is doing Joe a favour and feels pleased with himself. Pip is aware that Joe is not at ease in his company. Later

Pip talks to Biddy and learns that she intends to be a teacher now that her work at the forge is ended. They talk about Pip's sister and about Orlick who Biddy says she has seen lurking around. Pip says he intends to visit Joe often but is hurt when Biddy appears to doubt him. Biddy shows that she understands Pip better than he does himself when she doubts that he will return.

CHAPTERS 36–9 – The benefactor is revealed

1. **Pip is heavily in debt on his twenty-first birthday.**
2. **Herbert is helped in business.**
3. **Miss Havisham and Estella quarrel.**
4. **Pip's convict reappears.**

Pip and Herbert continue to run up debts. At last Pip reaches the age of twenty-one and, as he expected, he is summoned to Jaggers' office. Jaggers asks 'what do you suppose you are living at the rate of?' (Ch. 36, p. 287) and Pip has to admit that he does not know. He asks Jaggers if he is to learn anything about his guardian but Jaggers will not give him any information on this topic. Pip then asks if he is to receive anything whereupon Jaggers produces a five hundred pound note and tells him that this is to be his annual allowance from this time forward until his benefactor appears and that he will be responsible for his own affairs.

Pip decides he would like to help Herbert to get a start in business and he asks Wemmick for his opinion. Wemmick tells him that his office opinion is that he may as well throw his money in the river but that if he wants to know his Walworth opinion he will have to call on him at home.

> **CHECKPOINT 26**
>
> How does Pip show his generous nature at this point?

The following Sunday Pip goes down to Walworth and has tea with Wemmick, his father and Wemmick's friend, Miss Skiffins. Wemmick, when asked his advice about Herbert, says he will approach Miss Skiffins' brother with a view to finding Herbert an opening in business. Pip insists that this is to be done without Herbert's

Chapters 36–9 continued

knowledge. It is to Pip's credit that he is determined that some good should come out of his good fortune.

Gradually, with the help of Wemmick and Miss Skiffins' brother, Pip arranges an opening for Herbert with a young merchant. When Herbert arrives home with the news of his success, Pip is moved to tears at the thought that his expectations have finally done someone some good.

Pip's thoughts turn constantly to Estella and the house at Richmond where she is staying. His suffering is made worse because he knows that Estella uses him to tease her other admirers when he goes to visit her. He experiences nothing but unhappiness in her company but he still dreams of being with her for the rest of his life. One day Estella tells him that Miss Havisham wants to see her and that Pip is to take her.

At Satis House Pip is disturbed by the way in which Miss Havisham is eager to know all about the men who are fascinated by Estella. He sees that 'Estella was set to wreak Miss Havisham's revenge on men' (Ch. 38, p. 302). Deep down, Pip realises that the situation with Estella is hopeless but he cannot help himself and hangs on to the dream that they are intended to marry.

CHECKPOINT 27

How does Miss Havisham seem at this point in the novel?

Pip witnesses a bitter quarrel between Miss Havisham and Estella. Miss Havisham complains that Estella never shows her any love or affection, that she is ungrateful. She becomes more and more emotional about this. Estella coolly replies that she is very grateful to her mother by adoption but that she cannot give her what she was never given herself. She is entirely Miss Havisham's creation. Pip spends a restless night at the house and at one point sees Miss Havisham wandering with a lighted candle moaning to herself. Miss Havisham begins to realise she has created something terrible in her training of Estella.

Back in London, Pip and Herbert are at a meeting of the dining club when Pip takes great offence at Bentley Drummle's proposing a toast to Estella. Pip says that Drummle is lying when he claims to know her but Drummle is able to produce a note from Estella and Pip has to apologise. It depresses him further to find out that Drummle is pursuing her and is often in her company. Drummle's pursuit of Estella is a further torture to Pip. He cannot bear to see her encourage the clumsy ill-tempered oaf. One night at a ball, Pip challenges Estella about encouraging Drummle. Estella replies that she is only deceiving Drummle as she does others. Pip is the only one she does not deceive.

By the time Pip is twenty-three he and Herbert have moved to apartments in the Temple. One stormy night when Pip is on his own, as Herbert is abroad on business, he hears a footstep on the stairs. The description of the foul weather sets the scene for the arrival of the disturbing visitors. When he goes out with his reading lamp he finds a rough-looking man of about sixty who seems to be pleased to see him. Pip asks him his business and rather reluctantly invites him in. Pip then realises 'I could not have known my convict more distinctly than I knew him now' (Ch. 39, p. 316). The man kisses Pip's hands and goes to embrace him saying he has never forgotten him.

> **CHECKPOINT 28**
>
> How does Dickens use the weather to announce the arrival of Magwitch?

Pip is shocked and horrified as the man gradually discloses that he is his benefactor, that Jaggers is his agent. After serving time in Australia, the convict had made a great deal of money there and had rewarded Pip by having him educated as a gentleman. He had returned to England to see his creation even though he would be liable to be

CHECKPOINT 29

What does Pip now realise about his life so far?

EXAMINER'S SECRET

You will not get high marks simply by retelling the story.

hanged if he were caught in the country. Pip finds him repulsive but shelters him and gives him Herbert's bed. He then sits and thinks how all his ideas about Miss Havisham's plans for Estella and him were figments of his imagination and how he has abandoned Joe for the sake of a convict. He feels worthless.

Resolution?

Notice how the various strands of the story are beginning to come together at this point. The reader is left wondering how the following points will be resolved.

- Estella's parentage

- Miss Havisham's future

- Pip and Estella

- The role of Magwitch in Pip's life

- Orlick's hatred of Pip

- The other convict's relation to the main characters

As we move into the final part of the novel, all of the above plot elements are in place and the reader has to wait and see how these elements will be used.

Now take a break!

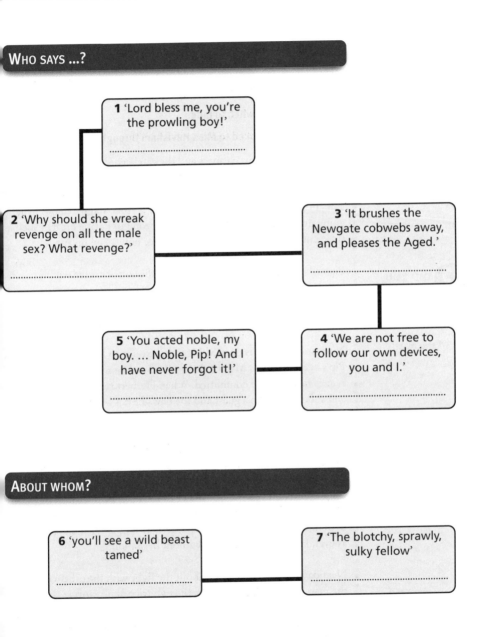

WHO SAYS ...?

1 'Lord bless me, you're the prowling boy!'

....

2 'Why should she wreak revenge on all the male sex? What revenge?'

....

3 'It brushes the Newgate cobwebs away, and pleases the Aged.'

....

5 'You acted noble, my boy. ... Noble, Pip! And I have never forgot it!'

....

4 'We are not free to follow our own devices, you and I.'

....

ABOUT WHOM?

6 'you'll see a wild beast tamed'

....

7 'The blotchy, sprawly, sulky fellow'

....

Check your answers on p. 89.

CHAPTERS 40–2 – Magwitch's story

1 **Magwich tells Pip his history.**

2 **Pip helps Magwitch to hide.**

3 **Magwitch is linked to Miss Havisham through Compeyson.**

Pip decides to tell his cleaners and the gatekeeper that the convict is his uncle. He is disturbed to find that someone has possibly followed the old man into the building. Next morning the convict tells Pip something of his background. His name is Abel Magwitch but he is going under the name of Provis. He is proud of having created such a fine gentleman in Pip and he wants to see him spend his money.

Pip calls on Jaggers who confirms that the convict is indeed his benefactor. Jaggers is very crafty saying 'That is the man, ... in New South Wales' (Ch. 40, p. 335). Pip's worries about Magwitch being discovered give him no time to dwell on his other problems.

No matter how he is dressed Magwitch seems to look like a convict in Pip's eyes. Pip finds Magwitch repulsive and he wonders what sorts of crimes he may have committed. When Herbert returns he is surprised and shocked by Pip's guest and the news he has brought. Magwitch makes him swear on the Bible to keep his presence secret.

Pip has arranged lodgings for Magwitch nearby and Herbert agrees that the most important thing is to get Magwitch out of the country. Pip feels that he cannot take any more of Magwitch's money and that his presence in England is a danger to them all. He realises that Magwitch will not leave the country without him so he resolves to go with him. Herbert agrees to help. Herbert is as loyal and dependable as ever. He agrees to help Pip without hesitation.

Next day Pip asks Magwitch about the fight with the other convict on the marshes and Magwitch tells the two friends his story:

- Magwitch has been in and out of jails all his life and does not remember his parents.

DID YOU KNOW?

A convict who returned from transportation faced the death penalty.

- Twenty years previously he became involved with a man called Compeyson, a swindler and forger who had been brought up as a gentleman.

- He became Compeyson's accomplice and when they were eventually caught, Compeyson saw to it that most of the blame fell on Magwitch who received a greater prison sentence.

- When Magwitch was free on the marshes and learned that Compeyson had also escaped he felt that the greatest revenge he could have would be to return Compeyson to captivity.

- Compeyson's punishment for escaping was light while Magwitch was transported for life.

> **CHECKPOINT 30**
>
> Why does Magwitch hate Compeyson so much?

Magwitch's story is of a sad, pathetic and brutal life. He sees in Pip something good which he has managed to create.

Herbert informs Pip that Compeyson was the man who abandoned Miss Havisham on their wedding day.

> **Coming together**
>
> Notice how Dickens is beginning to bring strands of the plot together: the convicts, Satis House and the 'expectations'.

CHAPTERS 43–5 – Estella is to be married

❶ Pip is distraught to hear that Estella is to marry Drummle.

❷ Herbert helps Magwitch to hide.

Pip feels he must see Estella and Miss Havisham one last time before he leaves the country with Magwitch. When he goes to Richmond he finds that Estella has gone to Miss Havisham's. This puzzles Pip as it is the first time she has made such a visit without his company. Next day Pip follows her. When he arrives at the Blue Boar he finds Bentley Drummle. They are rude to each other and neither mentions Estella but he hears Drummle announcing that he is to dine with a young lady that evening. Pip sees a man in the inn yard who reminds him of Orlick. Once again Pip feels the sinister presence of Orlick. It is not the first time that a man in dust-coloured clothes is mentioned. This is how the gatekeeper described the man who had followed Magwitch into the Temple.

CHECKPOINT 31

What change does Pip now see in Miss Havisham?

At Satis House, Pip accuses Miss Havisham saying 'But when I fell into the mistake, ... you led me on' (Ch. 44, p. 360) and she admits to this. He asks her to continue with the help he has given Herbert as he will not be able to do so. Pip achieves a certain dignity in his confrontation of Miss Havisham. He is able to think of others and enlists her help to further Herbert's career.

Pip tells Estella he loves her and has always believed that they were meant for each other. Estella tells him again that 'It is in my nature' (Ch. 44, p. 362) to have no feelings. When he says he has seen Drummle, Estella tells Pip that she and Drummle are to be married. Pip begs her not to throw herself away on such a stupid brute but she says the arrangements have been made and that she is unlikely to be a blessing to him. With Estella's announcement that she is to be married all of Pip's dreams are shattered. Pip is heartbroken and declares that he will never forget her. He gives a passionate account of his love for her.

Pip is so distraught that he walks all the way back to London. When he arrives at the gate of the Temple he is given a note from Wemmick telling him not to go home. Pip spends the night in a hotel but cannot sleep.

CHECK THE BOOK

Room at the Top (1957) is a novel by John Braine in which the hero is an unscrupulous young man who marries for wealth and social position.

In the morning he goes to see Wemmick at Walworth. Over breakfast Wemmick tells him that he heard some prison gossip about Magwitch's return from Australia and also that someone has been watching Pip and his benefactor. Pip also finds out from Wemmick that Compeyson is in London. Wemmick has informed Herbert of the danger and Herbert has arranged lodgings for Magwitch at the house near the river where his girlfriend Clara lives with her father. This will be convenient for secretly getting on board a ship when the time comes.

Tension mounts

The danger mounts for Pip and Magwitch with news that they are being watched and that Compeyson is in London.

> **EXAMINER'S SECRET**
>
> If the rubric gives planning time, **use it** to plan your answers!

CHAPTERS 46–8 – Estella's mother and Magwitch

① Magwitch prepares to escape.

② The other convict turns up.

③ Pip realises who Estella's mother is.

In the evening Pip visits Magwitch and is introduced to Clara who looks after her bedridden bad-tempered father. Notice how Herbert's happy relationship with Clara is a contrast to Pip's unhappy love for Estella. Magwitch has been lodged at the top of the house where he has a good view of the river. Pip tells him what Wemmick said 'about getting him abroad' (Ch. 46, p. 378) but decides to say nothing about Compeyson in case Magwitch is tempted to go after him. Pip feels a genuine concern for Magwitch and his better qualities are emerging. The convict agrees to Pip's idea that they should get out of the country and is pleased when Herbert suggests that Pip should buy a boat to row on the river. If they are regularly seen on the water no one will notice when they come down to pick up Magwitch.

Next day, Pip buys the boat and he and Herbert become familiar sights on the river. Pip cannot get rid of the feeling he is being watched nor forget his fears for the safety of Magwitch.

> **CHECKPOINT 32**
>
> Why is it important that Pip feels he is being watched?

Several weeks pass in this way while Pip awaits more news from Wemmick. One evening Pip goes to see Mr Wopsle perform in a play. During the performance Pip notices the actor staring at him. After the play Wopsle tells him he was staring at the man behind Pip and he was sure it was 'one of those two prisoners sat behind you tonight' (Ch. 48, p. 386). Pip realises that he means Compeyson. Compeyson's

CHECK THE BOOK

A Trampwoman's Tragedy (1902) is a poem by Thomas Hardy. The subject matter of the poem is very similar to the story of Molly. The poem can be found in *Chosen Poems of Thomas Hardy*, edited by James Gibson (1978).

presence behind Pip at the play is particularly mysterious and sinister. Dickens is building up the tension.

About a week after this Pip meets Jaggers in the street and is invited home to dine with him. He hands Pip a note from Miss Havisham who would like to see him about the business matter he had mentioned to her. To Pip's discomfort Jaggers brings up the subject of Estella's marriage to Drummle and proposes a toast that she will get the better of him. Pip notices Jaggers' housekeeper Molly standing nervously by and realises whom she reminds him of. Pip has had strange feelings about Jaggers' house and Estella for some time and now he realises that Molly is the connection. He becomes convinced that she must be Estella's mother.

Pip walks part of the way home with Wemmick who tells him that over twenty years previously Jaggers had defended Molly on a charge of strangling a woman. She was also said to have murdered her own child, a little girl of three years. After her release she had gone to work for Jaggers. Wemmick has nothing more to tell him and they go their separate ways.

> **More suspense**
>
> Notice how Dickens hints at further developments in the plot in order to build up suspense.

CHAPTERS 49–52 – The fire and the truth about Estella

❶ Miss Havisham is badly burned in a fire at her house.

❷ Pip finds out who Estella's parents are.

❸ Pip receives a mysterious letter.

Pip goes to see Miss Havisham on the following day and finds her sitting by the fire looking very lonely. She is full of remorse for what she has done and feels that Pip must hate her for it. He explains how she can help Herbert and she signs a note for Jaggers to release the money. She says 'If you can ever write under my name, "I forgive her," … – pray do it!' (Ch. 49, p. 398). Pip does forgive her.

Pip learns that Estella is now married to Drummle. In answer to his question Miss Havisham says she does not know anything about Estella's parents, only that Jaggers brought her to Satis House when she was two or three years old.

As he is walking through the garden and the brewery yard before leaving, Pip imagines he sees Miss Havisham hanging from a beam. He is so uneasy that he calls back to her room. She is sitting by the fire when suddenly her clothes are set alight and Pip throws first his coat over her and then the table cloth from the rotting wedding feast. She is badly burned and when the doctor arrives she is laid out on the wedding-feast table. Pip has received burns to his hands and arms. As he leaves, she is still regretting the harm she has done.

Back in London, Herbert looks after Pip. They both know how important it is that his hands should heal quickly so that he can row the boat when needed. Herbert tells Pip of a conversation he has had with Magwitch:

CHECKPOINT 33

What might the reader make of Pip's behaviour here?

CHECKPOINT 34

What does Miss Havisham realise at the end of her life?

- The convict told him how a woman he was involved with had been charged with murder and had threatened to kill their child.

- Pip realises he has been talking about Estella's mother.

- Magwitch believes that the woman carried out her threat.

- Pip tells Herbert that he is sure that Magwitch is Estella's father.

Pip is determined to find out the truth about Estella and next morning he goes to confront Jaggers about the matter. He tells Jaggers about the fire and Miss Havisham's injuries. He hands over the note concerning Herbert's money and is given a cheque. Pip then tells Jaggers that he knows who Estella mother is and that he believes Provis to be her father: 'Even Mr Jaggers started when I said those words' (Ch. 51, p. 410).

CHECKPOINT 35

How do we see a different side of Jaggers' character here?

Jaggers admits, in his cautious way, that he had taken in the murderess as his housekeeper and had controlled her violent nature. He had also given up her daughter for adoption to save her from the fate of so many similar children he had seen in the course of his business. Jaggers asks 'For whose sake would you reveal the secret?' (Ch. 51, p. 414) and explains that it would be better for everyone if Pip remained quiet. Jaggers reluctantly reveals that he too has feelings when he talks about saving the child.

One morning Pip receives a letter from Wemmick suggesting he makes a move in the next few days. He has not fully recovered from his burns and Herbert suggests they enlist the help of Pip's old fellow student, Startop, but to tell him as little as possible. Herbert and Pip look for a likely ship and decide upon a steamer bound for Hamburg. They will wait for this ship in some quiet place down river and row out to it so that Pip and Magwitch can get on board. They arrange to pick up Magwitch from his lodgings on Wednesday.

CHECKPOINT 36

What does Pip feel is the one good thing he has done since he was first told of his expectations?

When Pip gets home he finds an anonymous letter. The writer says if he wants to find out more about Provis (Magwitch) he is to come down to the 'limekiln' (Ch. 52, p. 418) on the marshes alone. Pip has very little time to consider this, so he goes to catch the coach and leaves a note for Herbert saying that he has gone to see Miss

Havisham. Pip realises he is not thinking clearly as he goes down to the marshes in response to the letter. As he sets out for the limekiln after dining at an inn; he becomes aware that he has lost the anonymous letter.

CHAPTERS 53–5 – Pip is caught in a trap

1 Orlick captures Pip and plans to kill him.

2 Magwitch is in danger.

Pip knows the marshes well and has no difficulty in finding the limekiln. He is attacked from behind, tied to a ladder against the wall and is in great pain because of his burns.

When his attacker relights the candle Pip discovers it is Orlick. Orlick tells him 'I'm a-going to have your life!' (Ch. 53, p. 425). He has always hated Pip and blames him for most of his misfortunes. He boasts of attacking Pip's sister but says it was Pip's fault for making him angry. He says he knows about Provis (Magwitch) and the plan to get him out of the country. He has been working with Compeyson and says that Magwitch will be taken.

? DID YOU KNOW?

Orlick is a typical malcontent character. He exists only to upset others.

GLOSSARY

limekiln a furnace where lime is produced

Orlick is about to kill Pip with a hammer when the door bursts open and Pip is saved by Herbert, Startop and the draper's boy from the town who has led the rescuers to the limekiln. In the struggle Orlick manages to escape. Herbert tells Pip he had found the anonymous letter on the floor of their lodgings and had been worried enough to follow him.

CHECKPOINT 37

How have Pip and Magwitch changed roles?

Back in London, Pip tries to rest and prepare himself for the escape attempt. On the Wednesday morning, Pip, Herbert and Startop take their boat from the Temple stairs and start rowing down river. They pick up Magwitch at Mill Pond Bank and carry on downstream. Magwitch is disguised as a river pilot. He seems the calmest of the party. Pip is resigned to the idea of going abroad with Magwitch. He feels he owes it to him.

After dark they stop at an inn on a deserted stretch of the shore and they spend the night there. Pip is uneasy and sees two men looking at their boat during the night.

Next day, they row out on the river to await the steamer. As the steamer approaches they are hailed from another rowing boat and Magwitch is called upon to surrender. When the other boat closes with them there is a struggle and Magwitch unmasks a man who is with the police. It is Compeyson. At that moment they are run down by the steamer. Pip, Herbert and Startop are pulled aboard the police galley but Magwitch and the other man have disappeared. As it turns out, the friends have been under observation all the time. The police and Compeyson have been waiting for them to make their move.

CHECKPOINT 38

How does Pip reveal the good side of his nature in the episode on the river?

Magwitch is later pulled from the river and manacled. He is badly injured and he tells Pip that he and Compeyson went under together but that he let go of Compeyson and swam away. Compeyson drowns. Pip stays with Magwitch as he is taken back to London and he promises not to leave him. Magwitch's trial for returning from transportation is set for a month's time. Pip shows strong loyalty towards Magwitch and compassion for him. He feels it would be better for him to die of his injuries than to be tried and hanged.

One evening Herbert announces that he will soon be leaving to run his firm's branch in Cairo. He offers Pip a job as clerk with the prospects of promotion to partner. Pip says he has too much on his mind to consider it clearly. His generosity towards Herbert has provided Pip with the possibility of a future career. He would not be entitled to any of Magwitch's money even if he wanted it.

On the day he says goodbye to Herbert, Pip meets Wemmick who invites him to take a walk with him the following morning. This turns out to be the day of Wemmick's marriage to Miss Skiffins and Pip is enroled as the best man. Afterwards, Wemmick asks Pip not to mention it at the office. The comic scene at the Walworth wedding provides a humorous contrast to the sad events in London.

> **CHECKPOINT 39**
>
> What moral judgement is made here about the profits from crime?

CHAPTERS 56–9 – The death of Magwitch

1. Magwitch is sentenced to death but his health deteriorates.
2. On his death bed, Pip tells Magwitch that his daughter is alive and beautiful and that he loves her.
3. Pip falls ill and is cared for by Joe.
4. Miss Havisham dies.
5. Pip decides to marry Biddy but arrives at the forge after she has just married Joe.
6. Pip goes to work abroad and returns eleven years later.
7. He meets Estella again.

During the next month, Pip visits Magwitch in the prison infirmary every day and sees him grow weaker. When Magwitch comes to trial, Pip is allowed to stand near the dock and hold his hand. The trial is a mere formality as it is obvious that Magwitch has committed the crime of returning. He is sentenced to death with thirty-one other prisoners on the last day of the Court Sessions. The mass sentence of death on thirty-two prisoners is a grim reminder of the legal system of the time.

Pip cannot rest and writes appeals and petitions to the Home Secretary and other important people on Magwitch's behalf. He continues to visit Magwitch and the convict's health steadily

> **CHECKPOINT 40**
>
> Magwitch is too weak to stand as he is sentenced to death. What does this tell you of British justice?

Chapters 56–59 continued

deteriorates. Pip shows great devotion to Magwitch in his final days. It redeems him in our eyes because he can gain no credit in polite society for being associated with a convict. When he realises Magwitch is about to die he tells him that his daughter 'is a lady and very beautiful. And I love her!' (Ch. 56, p. 460). Magwitch kisses Pip's hand before he dies. It is a very moving scene when Pip tells the dying convict about his daughter. It is the final stage in our coming to look upon him as a sensitive and vulnerable human being.

EXAMINER'S SECRET

This sentimental deathbed scene is typical of Victorian fiction. You could find parallels to it and refer to them in your answers.

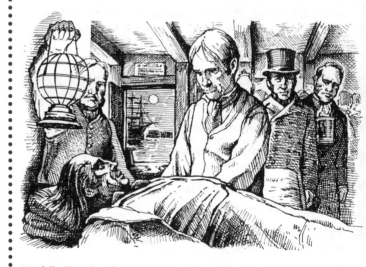

Pip falls ill and is almost arrested for debt. For a while he is delirious and when he comes to his senses he finds that Joe has been looking after him. Someone had sent a letter informing Joe and Biddy of his illness. When Pip enquires about Miss Havisham, Joe tells him that she has died. Her property has been left to Estella apart from four thousand pounds to Matthew Pocket, Herbert's father, and some small amounts to other relatives. He also tells him that Orlick is in prison for robbing Pumblechook.

Under Joe's care Pip gradually recovers. He tries to talk to Joe about his benefactor but Joe wants him to put the past behind him. As his health improves, Pip notices that Joe becomes more reserved with him and begins to call him 'sir' again. Pip is deeply touched by Joe's care of him but as he recovers we see that the relationship between them has been changed for ever by Pip's becoming a 'gentleman'. One morning he awakes to find that Joe has gone and has left him a note and a receipt for Pip's debt which he has paid off. Pip is determined to follow Joe and to tell him his true circumstances. He has also decided to ask Biddy to marry him. Pip is still taking things for granted when he assumes that Biddy will accept his proposal of marriage.

Pip stays at the Blue Boar and in the morning he walks by Satis House and sees that the property is being prepared for an auction. When he returns to the inn for breakfast he finds Pumblechook who patronises him to such an extent that he quarrels with him. Pumblechook accuses him of being ungrateful to the man who was the cause of all his good fortune.

When he goes to the forge he is puzzled because he cannot hear the sound of Joe's hammer and the forge itself is closed. Then he discovers Joe and Biddy in their best clothes and they announce that they have just been married. They are delighted to see him and Pip is only thankful that he never mentioned to Joe his own thoughts of marrying Biddy. He congratulates them both and says he going abroad soon and will work to pay off the money he owes them. He asks their forgiveness for his past behaviour and goes to see his old room before he eats with them.

Within a month Pip leaves the country and goes to work for Herbert. He gets on steadily and is able to pay off his debts. Eventually he becomes a partner in the firm.

Eleven years later he returns to visit Joe and Biddy at the forge. Pip is delighted to find that they have a little boy whom they have named after him. The following evening, thinking of Estella, he walks over to Satis House. He has heard that she led an unhappy life with Drummle but that she is now a widow. The house and brewery have gone and only the old garden wall remains.

As he is walking in the grounds he is surprised to meet Estella. She tells him that this is the first time she has been back. This piece of ground is all that remains of her property. She says she has often thought of Pip. She hopes they can still be friends even though they will be apart. Pip

CHECKPOINT 41

How do Joe's decency and simple dignity seem?

 DID YOU KNOW?

Dickens did not want the happy ending between Pip and Estella. He only used it because friends advised him that the original ending was too dark.

EXAMINER'S SECRET

Examiners **never** take marks away.

takes her hand and as they leave the garden he is convinced that he can see 'no shadow of another parting from her' (Ch. 59, p. 484).

Lessons learnt?

When they finally meet in the ruined garden of Satis House, both Estella and Pip have learned hard lessons from their experiences and are perhaps fit to make a future together.

This romantic ending is quite unlike much of Dickens' work and you need to consider the following about the future of Pip and Estella:

- Estella has been brought up to hate men. She knows no other way to behave and it seems unrealistic that she can change, even after eleven years.

- Pip's romantic ideals relate to the young Estella that he first met at Satis House when he was a boy. He does not know anything of the grown woman.

- Estella has already been married and is far more worldly-wise than Pip. This may well cause problems.

- Pip has no fortune and may well find it difficult to keep Estella in the style that she would want.

Pip's future may well not be a happy one, even though he has been reunited with his childhood love. Perhaps their expectations of one another are false rather than great.

Now take a break!

WHO SAYS ...?

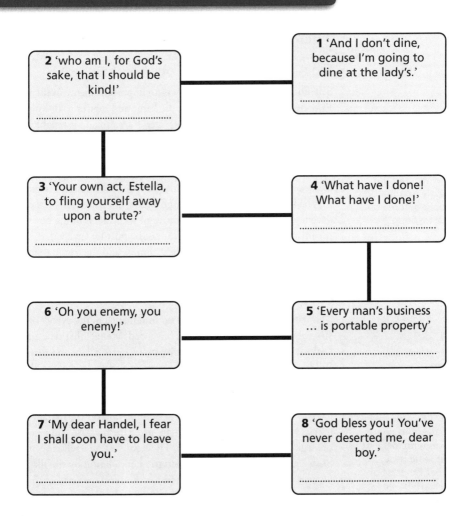

2 'who am I, for God's sake, that I should be kind!'

....

1 'And I don't dine, because I'm going to dine at the lady's.'

....

3 'Your own act, Estella, to fling yourself away upon a brute?'

....

4 'What have I done! What have I done!'

....

6 'Oh you enemy, you enemy!'

....

5 'Every man's business … is portable property'

....

7 'My dear Handel, I fear I shall soon have to leave you.'

....

8 'God bless you! You've never deserted me, dear boy.'

....

Check your answers on p. 89.

PART THREE

COMMENTARY

THEMES

SELF-KNOWLEDGE

Self-knowledge or self-discovery is an important theme in the novel. Pip rejects his humble origins at the forge and aspires to become a gentleman. Although he is given material wealth and is taught table manners and how to speak in a different way, he loses much in the process. It is only through hardship, loss and the example of Joe that he comes to humbly realise the worthlessness of his previous behaviour and the emptiness of his ambitions. Joe does not change. He realises that he is in his element at the forge and he never loses his basic decency and honesty. Estella is aware of what she is doing but makes the mistake of thinking that she cannot be hurt by such a destructive way of life. Her experiences with Drummle and the passing of time bring her to realise what she lost when she rejected Pip's love.

JUSTICE

There is an underlying theme of natural justice in the events of the story. Loyalty and goodness are rewarded. We feel that true and faithful Herbert deserves his happy marriage to Clara and that Joe and Biddy deserve their happiness together. We may also believe that Pip and Estella can be allowed a happy future when they have paid the price of their vanity and folly. Magwitch is an instrument of justice in his way. He tries to reward Pip for helping him on the marshes. He makes Compeyson pay the ultimate price for his past crimes, which the legal system had failed to do. The legal system itself is seen to be brutal, arbitrary, corrupt and open to manipulation by the likes of Jaggers. However Jaggers has tried to counter the effects of this system by saving one little girl, Estella, from its horrors.

HUMANITY

Human values are seen to prevail over wealth and position. Miss Havisham's wealth brings her no comfort at all. She uses it as a tool to upset her grasping relatives and to work her revenge on the male sex

EXAMINER'S SECRET
Always read the whole examination paper before you start writing.

CHECK THE BOOK
David Copperfield (1850) is a novel by Charles Dickens. It deals with many of the same issues as *Great Expectations* does. The hero learns important lessons by way of a series of relationships and experiences.

through Estella. Bentley Drummle has wealth but is a brutal and stupid bully, a worthless human being. Wemmick may talk about the importance of portable property but his greatest happiness lies in his warm human relationships and his simple pleasures in Walworth. Pip's wealth and position bring him no good at all except for the opportunity to help Herbert. The human values of Joe and the forge, of Wemmick's Walworth sentiments and of Herbert's love for Clara are those which bring happiness.

PRIDE AND REVENGE

Pride and the desire for revenge are shown to be extremely destructive. Miss Havisham feeds these destructive forces by keeping around her the reminders of her humiliation and betrayal. Her life is distorted. She lives in the dark and she ruins the lives of Estella and Pip through her selfish obsession.

STRUCTURE

The novel was finally printed in the three 'stages' that it is printed in today, but it was first published in weekly instalments. This means that *Great Expectations* does not have the structure of a conventional novel. Instead of moving towards a general climax, the story has many mini-resolutions of the plot. Each new episode needed a cliffhanger-type ending in order to ensure that the public would buy the next. This has often been seen as a weakness of Charles Dickens' novels as the story can become repetitive.

Great Expectations was originally published in the following instalments:

- Part One   Chapters 1–2; 3–4; 5; 6–7; 8; 9–10; 11; 12–13; 14–15; 16–17; 18; 19

- Part Two   Chapters 20–21; 22; 23–24; 25–26; 27–28; 29; 30–31; 32–33; 34–35; 36–37; 38; 39

- Part Three   Chapters 40; 41–42; 43–44; 45–46; 47–48; 49–50; 51–52; 53; 54; 55–56; 57; 58; 59

Charles Dickens was persuaded to change the ending of the novel. Originally there was to be no Chapter 59. The novel was to have ended with Estella remarrying after Drummle's death. There was to have been a short meeting between Pip and Estella some years later but no future for the two as a couple. This ending was preferred by Dickens as he felt that it was more realistic than a romantic one. He changed his mind after visiting his friend and fellow novelist Sir Edward Bulwer-Lytton. Bulwer-Lytton thought that the original ending was too disappointing and Dickens quickly wrote the ending that has subsequently been used in all editions.

In *Great Expectations*, Charles Dickens tells the story through the character of Pip. This is not as simple as it may at first seem. The Pip that tells the story is an adult who is thinking back on his life. When we are given information about Pip's childhood we are given it by the adult Pip. This is very important. Consider the differences between these two possible accounts:

- A child's version of the first day at school

- An adult's story about a child's first day at school

The accounts are likely to be very different indeed. All of the incidents in the novel are told to us by the adult Pip.

> **CHECKPOINT 42**
>
> How does Dickens make use of Pip as a narrator?

CHARACTERS

PIP

At the start of the novel, Pip is an innocent boy who has been brought up to respect his elders and betters. He is a kind-hearted child as is seen in the episode in which he brings the convict the file and the food. He is also rather gullible and really believes that a terrible man will tear his liver out while he sleeps unless he does as he has been told. This gullibility can be seen again when he visits Miss Havisham's house and is taken in by the charms of Estella.

Once he has met Estella he begins to change. Because she has referred to him as 'common' (Ch. 8, p. 60), he becomes dissatisfied with the life that he leads at the forge. Pip soon begins to feel that the life of a blacksmith is not good enough for him and he starts to be quite snobbish. When he finds out that he is to come into a great fortune, Pip is very quick to drop the people who had been his friends and family in case they embarrass him when he is a gentleman. He feels some pangs of guilt about this, but does it anyway.

Pip is eager to learn to become a gentleman. He is a good pupil but becomes a snob in the process. When Joe visits him, he does little to put him at his ease and is embarrassed by him and ashamed of him. He deceives himself as to his reasons for failing to call on Joe and Biddy on his visits to Satis House.

Wants to be a gentleman

Blind obsession with Estella

Obtains humility

He learns how to spend money freely and runs up large bills. He is aware, however, that he has encouraged Herbert to spend money he cannot afford and it is to his credit that he secretly arranges to help him in a business career. He later feels that this is the only good thing to have come out of his expectations.

His blind obsession with Estella and his belief that they are destined for each other continue until the latter is shattered by the arrival of his real benefactor and by Estella's marriage to Drummle.

By helping Magwitch, Pip demonstrates selflessness and compassion, and the truth about his good fortune and its origins brings him humility. He is prepared to return to the forge to make an honest living and believes he would like to settle down with Biddy. However, this plan is forestalled by Joe and Biddy's marriage and he goes abroad, convinced that he will remain a bachelor. His chance meeting with Estella after eleven years seems to offer the possibility of happiness after all.

JOE

Joe is a simple, honest blacksmith who has married Pip's sister. He acts as Pip's companion during the boy's early years and his clear, basic values make him stand out from the more devious characters around him. He loves Pip but never tries to stand in the boy's way, even when Joe is cast aside by the child he has helped to bring up.

Gentle
Honest
Faithful
Sensitive

Joe continues to be the decent and honest character that he was at the start. His simplicity and his language provide some of the humour in the novel but it is his kindness and his loyalty which shine through. He is always charitable in his response to Pip's neglect. He cares for Pip when he is ill but he knows that there is a gap between them which can never be fully closed since Pip has become a gentleman. He has a simple dignity and knows that he is seen at his best in his place of work.

We know he will be a good husband to Biddy and a father to little Pip. He deserves the happiness he has found and which Pip envies but does not begrudge him.

MISS HAVISHAM

Miss Havisham is a bitter old woman. She wants to take revenge on all men for the wrong that was done to her by one man. She sits in the clothes she should have worn for her wedding and is surrounded by decaying things in a darkened room. She has adopted a young girl, Estella, whom she plans to use to exact her revenge.

Miss Havisham delights in the way that Estella torments Pip and likes to keep her relatives guessing as to whom she will leave her money when she dies.

Bitter woman
Hates men
Uses Pip and Estella
Feels guilty at end

Miss Havisham continues with her plan to use Estella as an instrument of revenge on the male sex until she comes to realise she has created a monster. She accuses Estella of being hard and ungrateful but Estella says she cannot give her love as she was never given it herself. She tries to undo some of the harm she has done by helping Pip with his plan for Herbert and she leaves her cousin Matthew a legacy on Pip's recommendation. At the end of her life she is distraught with guilt for what she has done to Estella and to Pip.

ESTELLA

In the first stage of the novel, Estella is a beautiful young girl. She has been brought up as a young lady, but uses her education to talk down to Pip and make him feel inferior. Estella is cruel to Pip yet loyal to Miss Havisham. She is bitter and twisted due to the strange upbringing she has received from Miss Havisham. Estella does not fully realise that she is being used by the old woman and that she is, herself, little more than an agent for Miss Havisham's revenge.

Estella has been educated as an accomplished and sophisticated young lady. She warns Pip time and again that she has no heart and can never love anyone. She tells Pip that he is the only one to be so warned and that she makes fools of all the other men. She seems to become tired of this way of life and is almost self-destructive in her determination to marry such a brutal and ill-mannered man as Bentley Drummle. Even Miss Havisham tries to dissuade her. At the end of the novel, she is a widow and has little property left. Her hard experiences seem to have softened her, and she implies that she regrets having rejected Pip's love for her.

- Beautiful
- Heartless
- Educated
- Vehicle for Miss Havisham's revenge
- Humble at end

She is contrite and humble as she confesses that she realises what she threw away when she rejected Pip's love. She feels that the best she can hope for is that they can be friends. She is too humble to expect more.

ABEL MAGWITCH

At first, like Pip, we are repelled by Magwitch's coarse appearance and rough habits but as we learn of his awful brutal life we become more sympathetic towards him. His pride in the gentleman he has created is touching. Pip notices that his character softens and he forms a strong affection for the convict. Magwitch feels that Pip is a replacement for the child he lost. In a very moving scene, Pip tells the dying convict that his daughter is alive and is a beautiful lady.

Through Magwitch we are shown that the legal system in the early nineteenth century worked against the poor and uneducated. Compeyson was able to wriggle free while Magwitch suffered the full penalties for his crimes. Pip's loyalty towards Magwitch redeems Pip in our eyes.

- Led hard life
- Proud to have made Pip a gentleman

JAGGERS

Jaggers, a London lawyer, first appears in the novel when he meets Pip on the stairs of Satis House. He then visits the boy some years later to tell him that he is to come into a fortune. Jaggers knows all along who Pip's mysterious benefactor really is, but never gives the secret away.

Jaggers is king in the world of criminal law. Even the magistrates are frightened of him. Wemmick, his clerk, compares him to a steel trap. He is very careful never to commit himself and will not allow people to tell him things he does not want to hear. After the truth is disclosed about Magwitch and after Pip challenges him about the identity of Estella's parents, he does reveal a more human side to his character. He gave Estella for adoption because he felt moved to save at least one child from the fate of so many he had seen pass through the legal system. He also hints that he too may have had 'poor dreams' (Ch. 51, p. 412) when Pip refers to his own love for Estella.

Cautious
Cunning
'Steel trap'
Mysterious

HERBERT

Herbert is a perfect gentleman. He is tactful and kind when teaching Pip table manners. He is a true and honest friend to Pip, and a delightful companion, sympathising with his troubles, supporting him in his attempt to flee with Magwitch and saving his life at the limekiln on the marshes. He truly deserves to be happily married to Clara and successful in his career.

WEMMICK

Wemmick provides some of the humour in the novel, the dry lawyer's clerk who leads a double life as the whimsical architect and smallholder of Walworth. Even his employer, Jaggers, knows nothing of this Walworth life. Much of Wemmick's private life is devoted to looking after and entertaining 'the Aged' (Ch. 25, p. 208), his old deaf father. In London he is well-known as Jaggers' man and acts as an intermediary between Jaggers and his criminal clients. He shows great kindness towards Pip but likes to confine any personal business to Walworth. His great motto is: always look after portable property.

BENTLEY DRUMMLE

A fellow student at Matthew Pocket's. He shows himself to be surly, bad-tempered and unsociable. He is arrogant and a bully. Drummle is a rival for Estella's affections and he finally persuades her to marry him. After treating Estella very badly he dies in a riding accident involving a horse he has beaten.

ORLICK

Joe's assistant at the forge, Orlick is bitterly resentful of Pip once the boy becomes the apprentice. He has a hot temper and it is only Joe's superior strength that keeps him in check.

His sinister presence makes itself felt throughout the story. He also resents Pip as he thinks the boy has thwarted his attempts to woo Biddy and has caused him to lose his job at Miss Havisham's. Orlick is in league with Compeyson for some time and has helped him in his plot against Magwitch. He finally imprisons and nearly murders Pip, after having confessed to the attack on Pip's sister. He escapes when Pip is rescued. The last we hear of him is that he is in jail for robbing Pumblechook.

BIDDY

Biddy is an intelligent girl with moderate ambitions; she wants to be the local schoolteacher. She sees that Pip's ambition will bring him a good deal of heartache. She becomes Joe's housekeeper and eventually marries him. She resents the way that Pip neglects Joe and frequently acts as his conscience. In the early stage of the novel she might well be in love with Pip. Biddy is a good-hearted girl and she appreciates Joe's kindness and simple integrity.

PUMBLECHOOK

A moderately successful corn-chandler who visits the forge to see Mrs Joe in particular. He has the annoying habit of firing mathematical problems at Pip. Pumblechook is generally insufferable, pompous and opinionated. He delivers the message that Pip is to play at Miss Havisham's and thereafter becomes a local legend as the man who made Pip's fortune.

EXAMINER'S SECRET

Plan your answers then you won't repeat yourself.

CHECKPOINT 43

Why is Biddy important to the novel?

EXAMINER'S SECRET

If you are asked to make a comparison, use comparing words such as 'on the other hand', 'however' and 'by contrast'.

WOPSLE

He begins as the church clerk, but even then he is not satisfied with remaining on the sidelines. He is forever boasting that he would deliver better sermons than the vicar. Thwarted in his ambition to become a clergyman he takes to the stage in London where he enjoys mixed success in some rather odd performances. His greatest claim to fame is his version of *Hamlet* which is greeted with barracking and interruption by the audience. He means well but has little sense of his own ridiculous behaviour.

MRS JOE

Pip's older sister, she is married to Joe Gargery and has brought Pip up 'by hand' (Ch. 2, p. 7). She feels hard-done-by and both Pip and Joe are victims of her violent temper. She defers only to her relative Pumblechook, the corn-chandler. After she is attacked by Orlick she becomes a helpless object of pity.

LANGUAGE AND STYLE

Students make common errors when starting to talk about the writer's use of language. It is probably one of the more difficult aspects of literature. In this section you will be given some information about the language used by Charles Dickens and some pointers as to how to go about discussing it.

Dickens is famous for his use of language to describe people, places and features of landscape.

CHARACTERS

There are two major points to note about Charles Dickens' use of language to create characters in *Great Expectations*:

❶ Character names: the names of Charles Dickens' characters give an idea of their character. This is known as **characternym**. Consider the type of person represented by the following:

- Pumblechook – full of his own importance and rather foolish

- Jaggers – a strong willed man who is not to be crossed

- Wopsle – spends his time trying to be important, but his attempts fail in a humorous way

Other novels have characters such as:

- Mr Bumble (*Oliver Twist*) – an officious, 'bumbling' man who abuses the power of his position

- Mr Gradgrind (*Hard Times*) – a stern man who believes that people can be treated like machines

② Perhaps the most striking use of language in this novel comes in the form of speech. Charles Dickens is a master of characterisation and much of this is done through the way the characters themselves speak. Here are some examples of the way speech is used in the novel:

- Joe Gargery is made to seem endearing through his humorous manner of speech:

    'I'm oncommon fond of reading, too … Oncommon. Give me a good book, or a good newspaper, and sit me down afore a good fire, and I ask no better.'   (Ch. 7, p. 45)

- This conversation is about reading, but Joe can read little more than single letters:

    'Here, at last, is a J-O, Joe, how interesting reading is!'   (Ch. 7, p. 46)

- This technique of depicting speech **phonetically** (as it would be said) is also used to give a comic edge to Magwitch's words:

    'You young dog, what fat cheeks you ha' got. Darn me if I couldn't eat 'em, and if I han't half a mind to 't!'   (Ch. 1, p. 4)

and

    'I've done wonderful well. There's others went out alonger me as has done well too, but no man has done nigh as well as me. I'm famous for it.'   (Ch. 39, p. 317)

EXAMINER'S SECRET

The answer booklet contains enough paper for you to get top marks!

EXAMINER'S SECRET

An A-grade candidate can analyse a variety of the writer's techniques.

- When representing Wopsle's performance of *Hamlet* in Chapter 31, Charles Dickens uses a mock-heroic **style**. He deliberately writes about unimportant events as though they were extremely important. This is done to bring humour to the situation.

- Orlick is surly and rude when he speaks. This is important as he is to become one of the villains of the novel.

- Look at the way that Mr Jaggers often speaks as though he is putting a case in court even when he is simply engaged in conversation. This is not accidental. It is intended to make Jaggers a very serious character and to let the reader know that he would never betray a confidence.

SETTING THE SCENE

Charles Dickens uses descriptive language to convey the mood of a particular scene.

EXAMINER'S SECRET

Look at the way that weather and places are used in the novel. Dickens is famous for creating moods that reflect actions and characters.

- After Pip's meeting with the convict in Chapter 1, the landscape and the weather take on a sinister aspect that the boy has not noticed before:

  > The marshes were just a long black horizontal line then, … and the sky was just a row of long angry red lines and dense black lines intermixed.   (Ch. 1, p. 7)

  'Red' and 'black' are associated with danger and death. It is no coincidence that these are the predominant colours in the landscape immediately after Pip's encounter with the convict. This is an example of Dickens' use of **imagery**.

- Look closely at the following examples of the striking use of imagery in the novel:

  - Miss Havisham's rooms (Ch. 8 and Ch. 11)

  - Mr Jaggers' office (Ch. 20)

  - Wemmick's house and garden (Ch. 25)

When you find numerous similar images grouped together you need to consider why the writer has placed them like this. It is important to note that the reader's opinion of Mr Jaggers would be quite different if his offices were brightly lit, pleasantly furnished and full of frresh flowers.

- Once you learn to recognise the use of **imagery** you should be able to begin to discuss it in detail in your work. Good students will comment on such features of language in order to show that they are able to read at a high level.

All of these techniques combine to give a quality of richness to the writing in *Great Expectations*.

Remember the following points about any text you read:

- The writer started off with a blank page.

- Every word has been written - it is not real. (You could say that the text is a **construct**.)

- One form of words may be far more effective than another in getting across a particular idea or feeling.

- The writer set out to do something – not simply to fill the page – you have to identify what this aim was.

- You should discuss whether the writer has been effective e.g. is a frightening passage actually frightening?

- Finally, try to develop an appreciation for style. This can only be done by reading the work of different writers. You need to have your own opinion as to how good Dickens is at expressing ideas and emotions.

EXAMINER'S SECRET

Higher-level achievement begins at the point when you show you are aware of being marked.

Now take a break!

PART FOUR

RESOURCES

HOW TO USE QUOTATIONS

One of the secrets of success in writing essays is the way you use quotations. There are five basic principles:

① Put inverted commas at the beginning and end of the quotation.

② Write the quotation exactly as it appears in the original.

③ Do not use a quotation that repeats what you have just written.

④ Use the quotation so that it fits into your sentence.

⑤ Keep the quotation as short as possible.

Quotations should be used to develop the line of thought in your essays. Your comment should not duplicate what is in your quotation. For example:

> **Pip tells us how he came to be called Pip when he says:** 'I called myself Pip, and came to be called Pip' (Ch. 1. p. 3).

Far more effective is to write:

> **Pip tells us that because he could not pronounce his full name** 'I called myself Pip, and came to be called Pip' (Ch. 1, p. 3).

The most sophisticated way of using the writer's words is to embed them into your sentence:

> **The fact that Estella says that Pip has** 'coarse hands' (Ch. 8, p. 60) **and wears** 'thick boots' (Ch. 8, p. 60) **upsets him and shows us how insensitive Estella can be.**

When you use quotations in this way, you are demonstrating the ability to use text as evidence to support your ideas – not simply including words from the original to prove you have read it.

COURSEWORK ESSAY

Set aside an hour or so at the start of your work to plan what you have to do.

- List all the points you feel are needed to cover the task. Collect page references of information and quotations that will support what you have to say. A helpful tool is the highlighter pen: this saves painstaking copying and enables you to target precisely what you want to use.

- Focus on what you consider to be the main points of the essay. Try to sum up your argument in a single sentence, which could be the closing sentence of your essay. Depending on the essay title, it could be a statement about a character: Mr Jaggers is very careful to be exact in what he says, 'There is a certain tutor, of whom I have some knowledge, … I don't recommend him, observe; because I never recommend anybody' (Ch. 18, p. 140); an opinion about setting: I think that the churchyard surrounded by the lonely marshes creates an eerie atmosphere, especially as it is getting dark; or a judgement on a theme: The inhumane treatment of prisoners is an important theme in the novel. Pip treats a convict kindly and is rewarded for it, whereas the penal system treats the same convict very harshly.

EXAMINER'S SECRET
Always have a spare pen.

- Make a short essay plan. Use the first paragraph to introduce the argument you wish to make. In the following paragraphs develop this argument with details, examples and other possible points of view. Sum up your argument in the last paragraph. Check you have answered the question.

- Write the essay, remembering all the time the central point you are making.

- On completion, go back over what you have written to eliminate careless errors and improve expression. Read it aloud to yourself, or, if you are feeling more confident, to a relative or friend.

If you can, try to type your essay, using a word processor. This will allow you to correct and improve your writing without spoiling its appearance.

EXAMINER'S SECRET

Everything you write on your answer sheet is marked.

Sitting the Examination

Examination papers are carefully designed to give you the opportunity to do your best. Follow these handy hints for exam success:

Before you start

- Make sure you know the subject of the examination so that you are properly prepared and equipped.

- You need to be comfortable and free from distractions. Inform the invigilator if anything is off-putting, e.g. a shaky desk.

- Read the instructions, or rubric, on the front of the examination paper. You should know by now what you have to do but check to reassure yourself.

- Observe the time allocation – and follow it carefully. If they recommend 60 minutes for Question 1 and 30 minutes for Question 2, it is because Question 1 carries twice as many marks.

- Consider the mark allocation. You should write a longer response for 4 marks than for 2 marks.

Writing your responses

- Use the questions to structure your response, e.g. question: 'The endings of X's poems are always particularly significant. Explain their importance with reference to two poems.' The first part of your answer will describe the ending of the first poem; the second part will look at the ending of the second poem; the third part will be an explanation of the significance of the two endings.

- Write a brief draft outline of your response.

- A typical 30-minute examination essay is probably between 400 and 600 words in length.

- Keep your writing legible and easy to read, using paragraphs to show the structure of your answers.

- Spend a couple of minutes afterwards quickly checking for obvious errors.

WHEN YOU HAVE FINISHED

- Don't be downhearted – if you found the examination difficult, it is probably because you really worked at the questions. Let's face it, they are not meant to be easy!

- Don't pay too much attention to what your friends have to say about the paper. Everyone's experience is different and no two people ever give the same answers.

IMPROVE YOUR GRADE

Most students can immediately make some improvement in their grade by recognising what it is that they are being asked to do. All written tasks can be broken down into the following simple areas:

- What did the writer set out to do?

- How did the writer go about doing it?

- Was the writer successful?

WHAT DID THE WRITER SET OUT TO DO?

You should consider the first point before you begin to write any lengthy answer. You must try to grasp what the writer has set out to do. In other words, was Dickens simply telling a story or did he perhaps have other concerns?

There were many writers in Dickens' day whose work is no longer read so perhaps he was doing something a little different from his fellow writers. The plot of *Great Expectations* is quite complicated but it is the way that Dickens handles the various elements of plot that makes the novel interesting. Look at the way that one part of the plot is built up to the point where a major event is about to take place and then the scene shifts to another area of plot altogether. This control of tension – making the audience wait – is a major element of the writer's craft.

Remember: Dickens was a professional writer and he needed to please his audience.

EXAMINER'S SECRET

You are always given credit for writing your essay plans.

HOW DID THE WRITER GO ABOUT DOING IT?

Many students concentrate on the second point only. This results in a lengthy retelling of the story of whatever it is they have just read. There is nothing wrong with some account of the story but if this is all you do then you have carried out a fairly basic task. The plot of most great novels, plays and poems could be given to a class of eight-year-olds. They would then retell the story and draw a lovely picture. The skills shown by the eight-year-old students would not amount to much.

Remember: simply retelling the story is not a high-level skill.

WAS THE WRITER SUCCESSFUL?

When you do come to discuss the way that the writer went about achieving his aims there are some things that you need to do.

- Decide what it is you want to say

- Select the parts of the text that support what you want to say (see **How to use quotations** in **Resources**)

To reach the highest level you need to consider whether the writer has been successful. If you think Dickens set out to create believable characters, has he managed this? Do you think he intended us to feel some sympathy for Miss Havisham and, if so, has he made us feel it?

A higher-level answer will always contain the personal response of the student. Do not be afraid to say '**I feel that …**' or '**I believe …**'. You must of course have some evidence for what you suggest. There are people who still think the Earth is flat but there is pretty good evidence that it is not.

Each time you make a major point you should support it, either by giving an account in your own words or by using a quotation.

Two major elements of Dickens' language which tend to be seen by only the best students are his use of **imagery** and of conversation.

- You need to show how the use of imagery is responsible for creating particular impressions. For example, when Pip first meets

Miss Havisham (Chapter 8) he likens her to a waxwork in a fairground and a skeleton he has seen. He feels that:

> Now, waxwork and skeleton seemed to have dark eyes that moved and looked at me.   (Ch. 8, p. 58)

Dickens is using images that we already associate with certain ideas, in this case, death. He has not chosen to use bright pleasant colours to describe Miss Havisham. She is meant to seem disturbing and clearly very eccentric. By contrast, the beautiful Estella is first seen in the morning light.

- The offices of Mr Jaggers are gloomy and oppressive:

> Mr Jaggers' own high-backed chair was of deadly black horse-hair, with rows of black nails round it, like a coffin.
>   (Ch. 20, p. 164)

This reflects the dark and unpleasant nature of much of the lawyer's work.

Writers know these associations and play upon them for effect. Take the simplest idea of all – villain dressed in black; good guy dressed in white. Such basic images occur throughout the history of world literature. Good writers do not simply use such basic images. They are constantly looking out for new things to use as comparisons. You need to recognise that this is how writers work and include references to it in your written answers.

- Dickens is one of the greatest writers of speech and the way a character speaks often reflects his/her nature. Wemmick speaks quite eccentrically at home:

> 'Getting near gun-fire, … it's the Aged's treat.'   (Ch. 25, p. 208)

Wemmick's reference to his own father as 'the Aged' (Ch. 25, p. 208) and his speaking so proudly of his odd little house helps the reader to form an impression of him.

- Of course people in London did not necessarily speak like this. Dickens is exaggerating types of speech for entertainment, much in the way that some television dramas do today.

EXAMINER'S SECRET

Always check your answer when you have finished.

**EXAMINER'S
SECRET**

Keep an eye on the
clock so that you do
not run out of time.

THE EXAMINER'S VIEWPOINT

If we consider three levels of answer which can be called basic, better
and best you might find it useful to see the key features of these
answers from the examiner's viewpoint.

Basic

Students tend to re-tell the story no matter what the question is. Many
simple comments will be made without support, e.g. '**Estella is not
very nice to Pip**'.

An answer at the basic level is usually a series of such simple
statements and contains no real understanding of the thoughts of the
writer, in fact the writer is rarely considered at all.

Better

At this level students will pay some attention to the question that has
been asked and make some connected comments with support form
the text.

Statements will be more detailed and will largely be supported with
direct references taken from the text. This can lead to a rather
mechanical form of writing with a string of comments and quotations
one after the other. There will often be long passages of narrative that
are repeated for no particular reason.

**EXAMINER'S
SECRET**

Spend most time on
the questions that
offer most marks.

Best

The best candidates feel no need to tell the story. They realise that the
examiner has read the book. Such candidates are able to concentrate on
the specific demands of the question and are comfortable with the idea
that the book has been written with a purpose and audience in mind.

Quotations will often be integrated into the students' own writing
rather than tacked on afterwards. Above all there will be a sense of the
effects achieved by the writer.

Don't forget the things you need to cover:

- What did the writer set out to do?

- How did the writer go about doing it?
- Was the writer successful?

Good luck with your writing about Dickens.

SAMPLE ESSAY PLAN

A typical essay question on *Great Expectations* is followed by a sample essay plan in note form. This does not present the only answer to the question, merely one answer. Do not be afraid to include your own ideas and leave out some of those in the sample! Remember that quotations are essential to prove and illustrate the points you make.

What are the results of Miss Havisham's desire for revenge?

Look carefully at the question. The key word in the question is 'results'. You need to look at the effect that Miss Havisham has on those around her. Clearly this is going to mean Pip and Estella, but the Pockets and her other relatives have also had their lives affected by her treatment of them. You may find it useful to plan your writing in the following manner.

> **CHECKPOINT 45**
>
> Why is drafting an essay plan a good idea?

PART 1

We first see her in the semi-derelict Satis House. She has deliberately let the house fall into bad repair because of the disappointment of her wedding day.

PART 2

She feeds her revenge by never allowing herself to forget what had happened to her, for example:

- Wearing the wedding dress
- Allowing the wedding feast to rot around her
- Stopping the clocks at the moment of her abandonment
- Keeping daylight out of the house

EXAMINER'S SECRET

Short, snappy quotations are always the best.

She torments her greedy, grasping relatives, the Pockets. She uses Pip in this as she lets them believe that Pip is to be her heir and that they will get nothing.

PART 3

Miss Havisham adopts Estella and brings her up with the sole intention of exacting revenge on the male sex. No real thought is given to the way this will affect Estella. Initially she brings Pip to the house for Estella to practise on. This only hurts his feelings at first, but begins to change his life as he falls in love with Estella. It makes him ashamed of Joe and the forge.

PART 4

Miss Havisham knows very well that Pip thinks for a very long time that she is his benefactress. She also lets him believe that she intends him for Estella. This is cruel as Miss Havisham knows that Estella has been brought up to despise men and that consequently she could never make Pip happy.

PART 5

She begins to realise that she has created an awful person when she complains that Estella shows her no affection. When Pip declares his love for Estella she finally feels remorse for what she has done. To make amends she tries to delay Estella's wedding to Drummle.

PART 6

She helps Pip in his scheme to further Herbert's business career. On Pip's recommendation she leaves some money to Matthew Pocket, the only relative who told her the truth about her wedding.

PART 7

Having wasted more than half of her own life she finally regrets having partially destroyed the lives of Estella and Pip.

FURTHER QUESTIONS

Make a plan as shown above and attempt these questions:

1 Examine the development of Pip's character brought about by the changes in his fortunes.

2 Does Pip deserve such kind-hearted friends as Joe Gargery, Biddy and Herbert Pocket? Explain fully the reasons for your answer.

3 How do our views of Magwitch change in the course of the novel and what do you learn from this about Charles Dickens' attitude towards the penal system?

4 Many characters in the novel show that money is no replacement for personal relationships. Discuss this idea with reference to any two of the following:

- Miss Havisham
- Bentley Drummle
- Estella
- Magwitch
- Pip

5 Considering the history of Pip and Estella's relationship, is the happy ending convincing?

6 How effective is Dickens' use of the marshes and the River Thames in the story?

7 Comment on the ways in which Dickens uses dialect and individual speech mannerisms in *Great Expectations*.

8 What aspects of Pip's personality lead to his misinterpretation of Miss Havisham's actions?

9 The London of *Great Expectations* is not the London of Dickens' time. Say how far the novel is nostalgic in its approach to life in England.

10 How does the novel reflect the attitudes towards the punishment of criminals that were present in Dickens' England?

CHECK THE NET

Visit **www.bbc.co.uk** and search for Victorians. You will find a great deal of information about life in Victorian Britain. There is even a section on crime and punishment.

LITERARY TERMS

alliteration a sequence of repeated consonantal sounds which are close together. The matching consonants are usually at the beginning of words. Alliteration may be used to stress a point or to bring humour to what is being said

characternym a name given to a character which carries suggestions about that person's manner or appearance

construct an invention of the writer, crafted for a purpose

diction the writer's choice of words. You should consider why particular words have been chosen for a certain occasions and what effect the words have, either separately or together. When Pip asks Estella in Chapter 33 whether Mr Jaggers had any charge of her, she replies 'God forbid!' (Ch. 33, p. 270). This is very different to simply saying 'no'. The phrase 'God forbid' communicates clearly that Estella would hate the prospect of Mr Jaggers being responsible for her

imagery an image is a picture in words. There are two obvious kinds of imagery – **simile** and **metaphor**. Imagery is used extensively by writers, indeed it is difficult to say very much without using imagery

metaphor a description of one thing in terms of something else. When Mr Trabb presents a roll of

cloth to Pip, Charles Dickens writes that he was 'tiding it out' (Ch. 19, p. 151) on the counter. This is a metaphor; the cloth is flowing along the counter like the tide flows

pathos the depiction of events which evoke in the reader strong feelings of pity or sorrow e.g. the death of Magwitch

phonetically writing words as they are spoken, not in conventional spelling. Dickens uses this method to illustrate dialect – often with humorous effects

simile a direct comparison of one thing to another. When Pip is to be sent to Miss Havisham's for the first time he says, 'I was put into clean linen like a young penitent into sackcloth' (Ch. 7, p. 53). A simile will always contain 'like', 'as' or some other linking word

style how a writer says something. The poet Robert Frost said, 'All the fun's in how you say a thing'. The style that a writer adopts depends very much on his own personality and on what his intentions are. Charles Dickens has Pip adopt a mock-heroic style when reporting on Wopsle's *Hamlet*. This shows that Pip thinks the performance is poor and unintentionally funny

CHECKPOINT 1 The convict's threats are highly exaggerated and sound almost amusing.

CHECKPOINT 2 To establish that Jaggers is respected and feared, even by dangerous criminals.

CHECKPOINT 3 The convict is later to reappear as Pip's benefactor.

CHECKPOINT 4 Through the use of the brandy bottle with tar-water in it.

CHECKPOINT 5 Mrs Joe is something of a snob and wants to appeatr to be refined.

CHECKPOINT 6 Pip really thinks that he might be caught and Charles Dickens uses this to develop tension.

CHECKPOINT 7 She is dressed as for her own wedding which should have taken place many years ago.

CHECKPOINT 8 The bitterness of Miss Havisham seems to have affected her.

CHECKPOINT 9 Estella has made Pip feel he is common; he decides to acquire an education.

CHECKPOINT 10 So that we will recognise him later.

CHECKPOINT 11 Miss Havisham's relatives do not want to upset her in case she leaves them out of her will.

CHECKPOINT 12 Miss Havisham is prepared to allow him to be humiliated as practice for Estella.

CHECKPOINT 13 Pip is starting to feel that his simple life with the blacksmith is now beneath him.

CHECKPOINT 14 Dickens is telling the reader that Orlick is sneaky and likes to make trouble.

CHECKPOINT 15 Orlick becomes a thoroughly sinister character from this point onward. Dickens intends to use him again in the attack on Pip.

CHECKPOINT 16 In reality this could only have been carried out by Orlick.

CHECKPOINT 17 That Miss Havisham is preparing him to marry Estella.

CHECKPOINT 18 Pip does not see that her behaviour points to her lack of interest in his future.

CHECKPOINT 19 Even lawyers were prepared to cheat in order to win cases.

CHECKPOINT 20 The visit brings some humour and light relief before the introduction of Drummle and the housekeeper in the next chapter.

CHECKPOINT 21 Wemmick becomes warm and human when he goes home to Walworth.

CHECKPOINT 22 Jaggers realises that Drummle is trouble.

CHECKPOINT 23 Pip's self-deception is complete and he does not want to face the truth.

CHECKPOINT 24 The visit to the play is used as comic relief from the difficult subject of Estella which appears either side of it.

CHECKPOINT 25 Dickens is hinting at Estella's parentage, though he is playing games with the reader.

CHECKPOINT 26 In his desire to help Herbert in business.

CHECKPOINT 27 We begin to see Miss Havisham as a pathetic figure as she begs for Estella's affection.

CHECKPOINT HINTS/ANSWERS

CHECKPOINT 28 A storm precedes the arrival of Magwitch. The dramatic nature of the weather reflects the events of the story.

CHECKPOINT 29 When Pip discovers the real identity of his benefactor, he is faced with his own vanity and gullibility. His life has been guided by fantasy.

CHECKPOINT 30 Most of the blame fell on Magwitch because Compeyson seemed such a gentleman.

CHECKPOINT 31 As he leaves he has the impression that Miss Havisham regrets what she has done to Estella.

CHECKPOINT 32 Dickens is telling the reader that the escape attempt will not go smoothly.

CHECKPOINT 33 Pip gains dignity in his forgiveness of Miss Havisham.

CHECKPOINT 34 Miss Havisham sees the harm that she has done and is filled with regret.

CHECKPOINT 35 He reveals his decent motives for saving Estella.

CHECKPOINT 36 He has helped to establish Herbert as a partner in a business.

CHECKPOINT 37 Magwitch is strangely passive during the journey down river. Pip is now the man of action.

CHECKPOINT 38 Pip remains loyal to Magwitch, even though this could lead to trouble for Pip.

CHECKPOINT 39 Dickens seems keen to point out to his readers that no one can profit from Magwitch's money as Magwitch has broken the law.

CHECKPOINT 40 Even a very sick man could be condemned to death. This is meant to seem brutal.

CHECKPOINT 41 They are still a bitter reproach to Pip.

CHECKPOINT 42 The reader is often able to see things that Pip does not, such as it being unlikely that Miss Havisham is Pip's benefactor. This can add humour or develop tension.

CHECKPOINT 43 She represents the girl that Pip could have loved if he had not been so wrapped up in himself. She ends up settling for Joe but the reader feels that Biddy's life has been wasted.

CHECKPOINT 44 No! It is the quality of your answer - your insight into the way that the writer is working that will earn you marks.

CHECKPOINT 45 Planning your essay before you write it will allow you to organise your material and make sure that you address the question properly.

TEST YOURSELF (CHAPTERS 1–19)

1 The convict (*Chapter 1*)

2 Pumblechook (*Chapter 4*)

3 Joe (*Chapter 7*)

4 Estella (*Chapter 8*)

5 Biddy (*Chapter 17*)

6 Mr Jaggers (*Chapter 18*)

7 Pip (*Chapter 18*)

TEST YOURSELF (CHAPTERS 20–39)

1 Herbert Pocket (*Chapter 21*)

2 Pip (*Chapter 22*)

3 Wemmick (*Chapter 25*)

4 Estella (*Chapter 33*)

5 Magwitch (*Chapter 39*)

6 Molly (*Chapter 25*)

7 Bentley Drummle (*Chapter 26*)

TEST YOURSELF (CHAPTERS 40–59)

1 Bentley Drummle (*Chapter 43*)

2 Miss Havisham (*Chapter 44*)

3 Pip (*Chapter 44*)

4 Miss Havisham (*Chapter 49*)

5 Wemmick (*Chapter 51*)

6 Orlick (*Chapter 53*)

7 Herbert Pocket (*Chapter 55*)

8 Magwitch (*Chapter 56*)

NOTES

Maya Angelou
I Know Why the Caged Bird Sings

Jane Austen
Pride and Prejudice

Alan Ayckbourn
Absent Friends

Elizabeth Barrett Browning
Selected Poems

Robert Bolt
A Man for All Seasons

Harold Brighouse
Hobson's Choice

Charlotte Brontë
Jane Eyre

Emily Brontë
Wuthering Heights

Shelagh Delaney
A Taste of Honey

Charles Dickens
David Copperfield
Great Expectations
Hard Times
Oliver Twist

Roddy Doyle
Paddy Clarke Ha Ha Ha

George Eliot
Silas Marner
The Mill on the Floss

Anne Frank
The Diary of a Young Girl

William Golding
Lord of the Flies

Oliver Goldsmith
She Stoops to Conquer

Willis Hall
The Long and the Short and the Tall

Thomas Hardy
Far from the Madding Crowd

The Mayor of Casterbridge
Tess of the d'Urbervilles
The Withered Arm and other Wessex Tales

L.P. Hartley
The Go-Between

Seamus Heaney
Selected Poems

Susan Hill
I'm the King of the Castle

Barry Hines
A Kestrel for a Knave

Louise Lawrence
Children of the Dust

Harper Lee
To Kill a Mockingbird

Laurie Lee
Cider with Rosie

Arthur Miller
The Crucible
A View from the Bridge

Robert O'Brien
Z for Zachariah

Frank O'Connor
My Oedipus Complex and Other Stories

George Orwell
Animal Farm

J.B. Priestley
An Inspector Calls
When We Are Married

Willy Russell
Educating Rita
Our Day Out

J.D. Salinger
The Catcher in the Rye

William Shakespeare
Henry IV Part I
Henry V
Julius Caesar

Macbeth
The Merchant of Venice
A Midsummer Night's Dream
Much Ado About Nothing
Romeo and Juliet
The Tempest
Twelfth Night

George Bernard Shaw
Pygmalion

Mary Shelley
Frankenstein

R.C. Sherriff
Journey's End

Rukshana Smith
Salt on the snow

John Steinbeck
Of Mice and Men

Robert Louis Stevenson
Dr Jekyll and Mr Hyde

Jonathan Swift
Gulliver's Travels

Robert Swindells
Daz 4 Zoe

Mildred D. Taylor
Roll of Thunder, Hear My Cry

Mark Twain
Huckleberry Finn

James Watson
Talking in Whispers

Edith Wharton
Ethan Frome

William Wordsworth
Selected Poems

A Choice of Poets

Mystery Stories of the Nineteenth Century including The Signalman

Nineteenth Century Short Stories

Poetry of the First World War

Six Women Poets

Margaret Atwood
Cat's Eye
The Handmaid's Tale

Jane Austen
Emma
Mansfield Park
Persuasion
Pride and Prejudice
Sense and Sensibility

Alan Bennett
Talking Heads

William Blake
Songs of Innocence and of Experience

Charlotte Brontë
Jane Eyre
Villette

Emily Brontë
Wuthering Heights

Angela Carter
Nights at the Circus

Geoffrey Chaucer
The Franklin's Prologue and Tale
The Miller's Prologue and Tale
The Prologue to the Canterbury Tales
The Wife of Bath's Prologue and Tale

Samuel Coleridge
Selected Poems

Joseph Conrad
Heart of Darkness

Daniel Defoe
Moll Flanders

Charles Dickens
Bleak House
Great Expectations
Hard Times

Emily Dickinson
Selected Poems

John Donne
Selected Poems

Carol Ann Duffy
Selected Poems

George Eliot
Middlemarch
The Mill on the Floss

T.S. Eliot
Selected Poems
The Waste Land

F. Scott Fitzgerald
The Great Gatsby

E.M. Forster
A Passage to India

Brian Friel
Translations

Thomas Hardy
Jude the Obscure
The Mayor of Casterbridge
The Return of the Native
Selected Poems
Tess of the d'Urbervilles

Seamus Heaney
Selected Poems from 'Opened Ground'

Nathaniel Hawthorne
The Scarlet Letter

Homer
The Iliad
The Odyssey

Aldous Huxley
Brave New World

Kazuo Ishiguro
The Remains of the Day

Ben Jonson
The Alchemist

James Joyce
Dubliners

John Keats
Selected Poems

Christopher Marlowe
Doctor Faustus
Edward II

Arthur Miller
Death of a Salesman

John Milton
Paradise Lost Books I & II

Toni Morrison
Beloved

George Orwell
Nineteen Eighty-Four

Sylvia Plath
Selected Poems

Alexander Pope
Rape of the Lock & Selected Poems

William Shakespeare
Antony and Cleopatra
As You Like It
Hamlet
Henry IV Part I
King Lear
Macbeth
Measure for Measure
The Merchant of Venice
A Midsummer Night's Dream
Much Ado About Nothing
Othello
Richard II
Richard III
Romeo and Juliet
The Taming of the Shrew
The Tempest
Twelfth Night
The Winter's Tale

George Bernard Shaw
Saint Joan

Mary Shelley
Frankenstein

Jonathan Swift
Gulliver's Travels and A Modest Proposal

Alfred Tennyson
Selected Poems

Virgil
The Aeneid

Alice Walker
The Color Purple

Oscar Wilde
The Importance of Being Earnest

Tennessee Williams
A Streetcar Named Desire

Jeanette Winterson
Oranges Are Not the Only Fruit

John Webster
The Duchess of Malfi

Virginia Woolf
To the Lighthouse

W.B. Yeats
Selected Poems

Metaphysical Poets

THE ULTIMATE WEB SITE FOR THE ULTIMATE LITERATURE GUIDES

At York Notes we believe in helping you achieve exam success. Log on to **www.yorknotes.com** and see how we have made revision even easier, with over 300 titles available to download twenty-four hours a day. The downloads have lots of additional features such as pop-up boxes providing instant glossary definitions, user-friendly links to every part of the guide, and scanned illustrations offering visual appeal. All you need to do is log on to **www.yorknotes.com** and download the books you need to help you achieve exam success.

KEY FEATURES:

Details on how York Notes can help you

Menu Bar to help you find your way around the site

Details on how to download York Notes

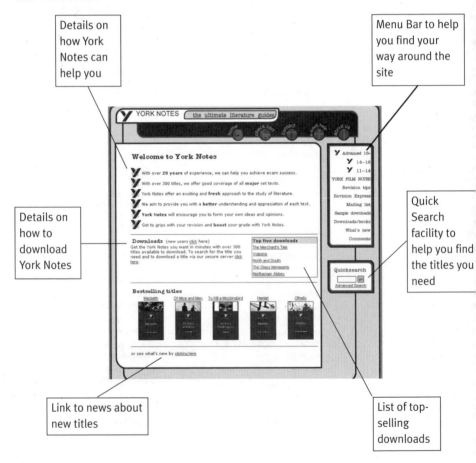

Quick Search facility to help you find the titles you need

Link to news about new titles

List of top-selling downloads